The LANGUAGE of SADOMASOCHISM

The
LANGUAGE
of
SADOMASOCHISM

A Glossary and
Linguistic Analysis

THOMAS E. MURRAY
AND THOMAS R. MURRELL

GREENWOOD PRESS
NEW YORK • WESTPORT, CONNECTICUT • LONDON

Library of Congress Cataloging-in-Publication Data

Murray, Thomas E. (Thomas Edward), 1956–
  The language of sadomasochism : a glossary and linguistic analysis
/ Thomas E. Murray and Thomas R. Murrell.
    p.   cm.
  Bibliography: p.
  ISBN 0–313–26481–3 (lib. bdg. : alk. paper)
  1. Sadism—Dictionaries. 2. Masochism—Dictionaries.
I. Murrell, Thomas R. II. Title.
HQ79.M87   1989
306.7′75′03—dc19   88–25099

British Library Cataloguing in Publication Data is available.

Library of Congress Catalog Card Number: 88–25099
ISBN: 0–313–26481–3

First published in 1989

Greenwood Press, Inc.
88 Post Road West, Westport, Connecticut   06881

Printed in the United States of America

The paper used in this book complies with the
Permanent Paper Standard issued by the National
Information Standards Organization (Z39.48–1984).

10 9 8 7 6 5 4 3 2 1

Copyright Acknowledgments

The authors and publisher would like to gratefully acknowledge the
permission of the following to use copyrighted materials:

Translation copyright © 1965 by Franklin S. Klaf, M.D., M.P.H. From the
book *Psychopathia Sexualis* by Richard von Krafft-Ebing. Reprinted with
permission of Stein and Day Publishers.

Havelock Ellis, *Studies in the Psychology of Sex, Vol III*, 2nd ed. revised
and enlarged, F. A. Davis, Philadelphia 1926. Reprinted by permission of
copyright holder and literary executor Francois Lafite.

*This book is respectfully dedicated to the memory
of Richard von Krafft-Ebing, Havelock Ellis, and Sigmund Freud,
who legitimized the scholarly study of sadomasochism,
and
to the memory of David W. Maurer,
whose pioneering work in the study of underground argots
continues to serve as an inspiration to linguists everywhere.*

Contents

Preface

The acknowledged leader in the study of underworld language was for years David W. Maurer, and rightly so: his research into the argot of criminals, spivs, racketeers, prostitutes, tramps, and a number of other cultural subgroups is unsurpassed in the light it has shed on language, culture, and how the two are inexorably related. But Maurer and, indeed, every other researcher in the field of underworld jargon have overlooked one important group of people and their language—sadomasochists. This oversight is made all the more conspicuous by a growing body of research from anthropologists, psychologists, sociologists, and other social scientists into sadomasochism and the various people who practice it.

It is for precisely this reason that the authors of this volume undertook the present research. The investigation began in the fall of 1986 when, following a lecture by Murray on the role of cant, argot, and jargon in linguistic variation, Murrell came forward and asked whether the kinds of heavily coded language he had noticed in a local newspaper qualified as argot. What followed was a year of data collection, personal interviews, and general surveyance of the subculture of sadomasochism and its language, the culmination of which is this book.

We have chosen to present the results of our research in three sections. The Introduction covers sadomasochism's history as well as its professional study and its occurrence in literature—our intention being not only to provide readers with a firmer grasp of exactly what sadomasochism is, how long it has existed, and how it has been studied, but to provide some understanding of how the subculture has produced the language it has. The body of the book consists of (1) a summary of our data-gathering methods and an explanation of how we decided what to include under the rubric "language of sadomasochism"; (2) a comprehensive glossary of over 800 terms currently in use by sadomasochists, with each citation containing full part-of-speech labels, etymologies, definitions, examples of usage, and ancillary notes; and (3) a brief substantive analysis of the glossary, in which we attempt to answer questions pertaining to how the language of sadomasochism is related to the subculture that uses it as well as to the English language as a whole. Following this are an epilogue occasioned by new institutional developments in the subculture; a section of endnotes; a list of references that includes all the published sources used in the preparation of this work; an appendix containing a select bibliography of scholarly and popular writing on sadomasochism; and, finally, a comprehensive, cross-referenced index to the synonyms in the language of sadomasochism. Although this project has been entirely a joint effort, Murrell has assumed primary responsibility for the Introduction and Murray for the glossary.

A number of other people have played a role in this project, and this is our chance to thank them publicly. First, three graduate students at Ohio State University—Ray Brown, Elizabeth Graham, and Inez Vaher—provided immeasurable help in the gathering of data: Ray pored over copies of magazines devoted to sadomasochism until his eyes were bloodshot; Elizabeth spent countless hours in libraries checking and rechecking secondary references; and Inez ventured into adult bookstores and clubs the likes of which most people could never appreciate. Second, the people interviewed for this research—from members of the vice squad in the Columbus Police Department to Briar Rose (an S and M women's support group located in a suburb of Columbus, Ohio) to professional dominatrices to anonymous individuals in bars and bookstores—provided us with original material without which our study would be sadly incomplete. Finally, and perhaps mostly, to the colleagues, friends, and relatives who, upon asking us what we were working on, heard "The language of, um, sadomasochism" in response, we offer our warmest thanks for understanding why the work had to be done, or at least tolerating us while we did it. We understand all the raised eyebrows and curious glances, and hope that this book will help to explain what we were doing.

The LANGUAGE of SADOMASOCHISM

Introduction: Sadomasochism— the Subculture and Its Place in History and Literature

For the overwhelming majority of humans, sadistic and masochistic behavior conjures up frightful images: the Nazi concentration camps of Adolf Hitler, the tortures of the Spanish Inquisition or the English Star Chamber, the murderous ways of the Hillside Strangler of Southern California, the relentless dripping of the Chinese water torture, or any of a number of unthinkably cruel acts documented annually by Amnesty International. In fact, the very idea of being a powerless captive forced to endure hideous torments at the hands of a cruel captor—or, conversely, imagining oneself as the administrator of physical or psychological torture to a fellow human—represents for most people the worst possible fate. And whenever such a person is discovered—a person for whom, perhaps, such behavior is not only acceptable, but enjoyable—he or she is accorded neither sympathy nor understanding by the rest of society; whether the person is a holdover from Hitler's Nazi regime or a respected Madison Avenue stockbroker, wanton cruelty is not the kind of behavior we, as a humane society, wish to tolerate in our fellow humans.

Yet there are some people for whom sadism and masochism provide the (perhaps necessary) framework for successful sexual relationships. *Within certain definable and negotiable boundaries*, sexual sadomasochists will seek out opportunities to give or receive pain. Richard von Krafft-Ebing gave us the names by which we still designate these people when he called the giver of pain for pleasure a "sadist"—after the Marquis de Sade—and the seeker of pain for pleasure a "masochist"—after Leopold von Sacher-Masoch. And although sadomasochism has been studied both as a social and as an individual behavior since Krafft-Ebing's seminal work, *Psychopathia Sexualis*, was first published in 1885, no one has been able to shake either the names he gave to these behaviors or the negative "whips and chains" connotations those names carry as psychopathic sexual acts.

Sigmund Freud, Richard von Krafft-Ebing, and Havelock Ellis set the tone and defined the parameters for studying sadomasochism in isolated cases of deviant behavior. All three studied not only sadomasochism, but, indeed, all forms of deviant behavior—nonsexual as well as sexual—as phenomena in isolation from that of the normative standards of the cultures in which their subjects lived. To Freud, Krafft-Ebing, Ellis, and their followers, behaviors that deviated from the accepted norms of a society were destructive of the individuals who engaged in them; in studying such phenomena, the early students of human behavior sought to find a cure or cures that would allow their subjects to resume, or perhaps enter into for the first time, a more normal life through the elimination of the deviant behaviors and the substitution of more normative behaviors for the deviant ones.

Following World War II, scientists and scholars from a variety of fields began to examine human behavior—including sexual behavior—not in terms of normal versus deviant, but in terms of defining *normal* and *deviant* quantitatively. Alfred C. Kinsey, who established the Institute for Sex Research at Indiana University in Bloomington, published the first two detailed studies of human sexual behavior from this quantitative viewpoint: *Sexual Behavior in the Human Male* (1948), and *Sexual Behavior in the Human Female* (1953). The effect of these two works on the study of human behavior, both sexual and otherwise, was to broaden the concept of normal behavior to include behaviors previously considered deviant but that were practiced by statistically significant portions of the human population. Subsequent work has further defined and refined Kinsey's categories, of course, but all such work has taken as fundamental assumptions the notions that, first, deviant behaviors are practiced by groups of people, not merely isolated individuals; second, what is considered normal behavior within these groups may differ from cultural or societal norms; and third, in spite of the second assumption, the behavior still remains within a normative range in the practicing group as a whole.

In parallel with these psychological studies of human behavior, sociologists and anthropologists began studying how human beings interact within definable cultural groups. Two of the most important discoveries they made are that small groups always exist within larger groups and that these subgroups establish and maintain separate, sometimes even clandestine identities within the larger groupings. These subgroups, or subcultures, tend to have many, if not all, of the trappings of a main culture—mode of dress, language, literature, art, rules of behavior—yet they also remain a part of the larger culture. As a result of this socio-anthropological work, we no longer think of cultures as monolithic social entities in which all members dress, think, or act alike; rather, we think of main cultures as being composed of multiple subcultures: a Hispanic subculture, a black subculture, a gay subculture, a Jewish subculture, and so forth. It seems that whenever groups of people identify with the same guidelines for dress, language, behavior, or organization, or when they share a common social, ethnic, economic, religious, or sexual identity, they form a distinct group within the overall group to which they belong. They form, in short, a subculture.

Recent work in the study of sexual subcultures in the United States has uncovered the existence of the sadomasochistic subculture. This subculture cuts across most, if not all, cultural and subcultural boundaries, and it encompasses all those people who derive some measure of sexual satisfaction from depictions of and participation in activities in which the giving and receiving of pain can lead to sexual satisfaction either directly or as a prelude to sexual intercourse. Sexual sadomasochists are homosexual, heterosexual, or bisexual; they come from a variety of social, economic, racial, ethnic, geographic, and religious backgrounds; and they seek out others who share their predilections for their mutual satisfaction. Both to find other practitioners of sadomasochistic sex and to communicate their specific sexual desires to potential partners, members of the sadomasochistic community have developed a highly diversified language within the language of the main culture. We will catalogue and explain this language in the second and third sections of this book; suffice it to say here merely that this language is so structured as to clearly inform other sadomasochists of a member's presence, preferences, and limits, while at the same time protecting the member from unwanted discovery by nonmembers of the subculture.

It is impossible to determine with any certainty how large the sadomasochistic subculture is. As Andreas Spengler points out (Weinberg and Kamel 1983, 58)—and our own research confirms—it is extremely difficult to find admitted sexual sadomasochists to interview: "Heterosexual sadomasochists live undercover; their groups are cut off from the outside world. . . . Only homosexual sadomasochists appeared to be approachable for investigation. Anonymity is one of the special norms of the sadomasochistic subculture." However, the statistics that have been developed in the past thirty-five years do serve to mark the outer limits and something of the inner composition of this subculture. The 1953 Kinsey study claims that 10 percent of males and 3 percent of females are "definitely or frequently aroused" by sado-masochistic stories, while an additional 12 percent of males and 9 percent of females admit to "some arousal" from sa-domasochistic stories (Kinsey et al. 1953, 677).

In 1979, Jay and Young published statistics in *The Gay Report* claiming that 9 percent of lesbians respond positively to the idea of sadomasochistic sexual activity, with 11 per-cent responding positively to "bondage and discipline"—a subcultural term that is sometimes used to mean a specific kind of sadomasochistic activity (see glossary) and is some-times used euphemistically to mean "general sadomasoch-ism." Among gay men, Jay and Young report that 15 percent respond positively to bondage and discipline, while 14 per-cent respond positively to sadomasochism. The researchers went on to ask their respondents how many of them engaged in sadomasochistic activity and in what frequency. Ten per-cent of the gay men admitted to engaging in sexual sado-masochism "with some frequency"; 7.5 percent said they engaged in bondage and discipline "with some frequency." Of the lesbians responding to the survey, 2.5 percent ad-mitted to "some frequency" of sadomasochistic sexual activ-ity, with the same number admitting to the practice of bondage and discipline. As we noted earlier, no reliable data yet exist on the overall percentage of the heterosexual pop-ulation engaged in sexual sadomasochism; however, there is no evidence to suggest that heterosexuals respond to sa-domasochism any differently than homosexuals.[1]

Andreas Spengler's study of German males who admit some involvement in sadomasochism reveals that there is no single type of individual with a particular sexual orientation who engages in, or is interested in engaging in, sadomaso-chistic sexual activity. Thirty percent of those responding to Spengler's questionnaire indicated that they were exclusively heterosexual in their orientation; at the other end of the spectrum, 38 percent of sexually sadomasochistic males in-dicated that they were exclusively homosexual. Spengler also gathered extensive demographic data that seem to suggest that no single sociological factor distinguishes the male sa-domasochist from his nonsadomasochistic counterpart.[2]

All of these studies suffer statistically because they rely on the responses of people who are reluctant to reveal themselves to an often hostile world. In fact, with the exception of the Kinsey studies, all of the statistics available rely on members of the sadomasochistic subculture coming forward with answers to the questions asked. Nevertheless, it is apparent from these few studies that a substantial number of human beings are either involved in or interested in sexual sadomasochism. Though sexual sadomasochists are a private group, a group living in the midst of larger and more influential cultures, they are definitely *not* a fringe group composed of outcast miscreants and malcontents, but a group representing the entire spectrum of human life.

An understanding of the language of the sadomasochistic subculture requires an understanding of how sexual sadomasochism differs from behaviors that it resembles in the larger world. When the sexual sadomasochist uses the word *torture*, for example, he or she does not mean the inflicting of serious or permanent or life-threatening harm by one human on another. To the sexual sadomasochist, torture involves both the sadist and the masochist in a contract whereby both will engage in activities that *will* bring real pain to the masochist—but it is a pain that both agree to keep within certain negotiated limits.[3] The sexual sadomasochist abhors true slavery, true kidnapping, true torture, and true rape as crimes against human dignity fully as much as the nonsadomasochist does.

John Alan Lee, in his article "The Social Organization of Sexual Risk" (Weinberg and Kamel 1983, 188), gives perhaps the clearest understanding of the difference between what he calls "true sadism" and "true masochism" (not to be confused with the *true sadism* and *true masochism* listed in the glossary) and the sadomasochism practiced by members of the sadomasochistic subculture: "True sadism would involve the desire to hurt and punish the partner without regard for the partner's pleasure. True masochism would involve the desire to be hurt, without regard for the master's conscience or enjoyment." In Lee's view, sexual sadomasochism involves both "wise practitioners" and "willing victims" in a kind of role-playing activity that both people enter into for the mutual gratification of each other. It is an activity more suited to the theater, in which the players take on roles—roles that they may trade in another encounter—for the specific purpose of giving and receiving pleasure mutually through the medium of the giving and receiving of pain. This key aspect of sadomasochistic sexual activity distinguishes it, in the minds of its practitioners, from the horrific crimes of a Gestapo guard or a Hillside Strangler or any common rapist or kidnapper, and hence cannot be stressed too much. It is the controlled context as much as anything else that defines the member of the sadomasochistic subculture and delineates him or her from the true sadist or true masochist.

The origins of sadomasochism as a form of sexual release, much less as a sexual subculture with its own language and modes of behavior, are lost in remote human history. Even a cursory reading of that history and the literature its people have produced, however, shows that both sadism and masochism have been a part of human behavior for as long as humans have recorded that behavior. Greek mythology contains the graphic tortures of Prometheus, chained to a rock while a bird plucks eternally at his liver; and the torture of Tantalus—a man tormented by food and drink ever present in his vision while ever just out of his grasp—has given to the English language the word *tantalize*. In the Roman Empire, the common punishment for misdeeds by slaves was public flogging; the common capital penalty for misdeeds by slaves was public crucifixion. And Christian tradition abounds in tales of the early martyrs suffering horrible torture and death at the hands of the Romans.

Human history contains abundant evidence of the public punishment of miscreants, and the history of the legal administration of justice reveals that most of our laws for deciding disputes, both between individuals and between the state and individuals, have some foundation in ancient laws and practices in which the use of torture and trial by ordeal prevailed. To call torture "sadomasochism," however, requires us to find evidence that the practices were entered into or observed by people whose primary interest was in the pleasure they could derive from these practices. If the surviving documentation does not specifically state that someone derived or sought to derive sexual pleasure from the infliction or reception of pain, we can only infer, either from the subject matter in the document or its manner of presentation, that sadomasochism might or might not have been a motivating force in the incident. Still, while the historical record may be spotty or subject to a variety of interpretations, enough unambiguous evidence exists to suggest that sadomasochism may have been an integral part of human culture since the beginning of the species.

Havelock Ellis, citing Wiedemann's *Popular Literature in Ancient Egypt*, presents what may be the oldest surviving masochistic utterance: "Oh! were I made her porter, I should cause her to be wrathful with me. Then when I did but hear her voice, the voice of her anger, a child shall I be for fear" (Ellis 1942, 112–13, n. 5). These lines, taken from an ancient Egyptian love song, represent a kind of masochistic love in which the male desires to be subjugated by his beloved so that he might experience pleasure when she treats him as a lowly slave. As Ellis says, "The activity and independence of the Egyptian women at the time may well have offered many opportunities to the ancient Egyptian masochist" (1942, 113).

Ellis also notes that in the *Satyricon* of Petronius, some courtesans, presumably Greek, dedicated whips, bridles, and spurs as votive offerings to the love goddess Venus—"tokens," Ellis calls them, "of their skill in riding their lovers" (1942, 132). Ellis admits, however, that these tokens could be explained in more than one way. Whips, bridles, and spurs are certainly elements of sadomasochistic play in which the submissive partner acts the part of a dumb animal for the dominant partner; indeed, many kinds of modern sadomasochistic activity involve the submissive being treated like a horse. Still, the possibility remains that these offerings to the goddess of love were symbolic of love relationships in which the women dominated but did not actually ride or whip their lovers.

Havelock Ellis was not alone in his inability to find incontrovertible proof of sadomasochism in classical times. Ellis (1942, 132) cites a remark from Eulenburg, in *Sadismus und Masochismus*:

> We naturally know nothing of the feelings of the priestess of Artemis at the flagellation of Spartan youths; or what emotions inspired the priestess of the Syrian goddess under similar circumstances; or what the Roman Pontifex Maximus felt when he castigated the exposed body of a vestal (as described by Plutarch) behind a curtain.

Both Eulenburg and Ellis were very careful not to appear to read too much into the ancient writers; both men, however, by including the scenes—sometimes in quite graphic detail—imply that such activity may have had more behind it than the obvious religious ritual in which such flagellations were practiced.

Richard von Krafft-Ebing, in *Psychopathia Sexualis*, devotes several introductory pages to a discussion of the similarity in motivations that exists in both religious practices and amatory activity as a foundation for his discussion of the ways in which normal emotional and physical processes become altered in what he terms "psychopathic sexual activity." In a particularly lucid passage (1965, 5), he says:

> Religion as well as sexual love is mystical and transcendental. In sexual love the real object of the instinct, i.e., propagation of the species, is not always present in the mind during the act, and the impulse is much stronger than could be justified by the gratification that can possibly be derived from it. Religious love strives for the possession of an object that is absolutely ideal, and cannot be defined by experimental knowledge. Both are metaphysical processes which give unlimited scope to imagination.

We are not suggesting any more than Ellis or Krafft-Ebing that religious practices—either of ancient Greece or Rome or of modern Christianity—are the foundations of modern sadomasochism. However, both Ellis and his sources, as well as Krafft-Ebing, noted the prevalence of flagellation in medieval Christianity and speculated that it was the precursor to modern sadomasochism. And if flagellation in Christianity inspired flagellation in sexual life outside of religion, it seems quite possible that flagellation in Greek or Roman or Syrian religious ceremonies might have led to flagellation in their sexual lives as well.

Havelock Ellis conducted extensive research into the origins of sadomasochism, and he had this to say about the use of whipping as a religious penance in the Catholic Church (1942, 129):

> Whipping has always been a recognized religious penance; it is still regarded as a beneficial and harmless method of chastisement; there is nothing necessarily cruel, repulsive, or monstrous in the idea or the reality of whipping, and it is perfectly easy and natural for an interest in the subject to arise in an innocent and even normal child, and thus to furnish a germ around which, temporarily at all events, sexual ideas may crystallize.

Ellis also noted, interestingly, that the religious chastisements meted out were performed on nude—or at least partially nude—penitents, "the humiliation thereby caused being pleasant in the sight of God" (1942, 129).

One final word from Havelock Ellis seems to make the case—as well as it can be made—that there is some link between religious penitence and sexual sadomasochism (1942, 130):

> The association of religious flagellation with perverted sexual motives is shown by its condemnation in later ages by the Inquisition, which was accustomed to prosecute the priest who, in prescribing flagellation as a penance, exerted it personally, or caused it to be

inflicted on the stripped penitent in his presence, or made a woman penitent discipline him. . . . There seems even to be some reason to suppose that the religious flagellation mania which was so prevalent in the later Middle Ages . . . may have had something to do with the discovery of erotic flagellation, which at all events in Europe, seems scarcely to have been known before the sixteenth century. It must, in any case, have assisted to create a predisposition. The introduction of flagellation as a definitely recognized sexual stimulant is by Eulenburg, in his interesting book, *Sadismus und Masochismus*, attributed to the Arabian physicians.

The apparent ease with which religious chastisement could be replaced by a less exalted motive is revealed by the number of times the Church felt compelled to react against flagellation in public. According to Ellis, in the eighth century Pope Adrian IV "forbade priests to beat their penitents." He also notes (1942, 132) an "epidemic of flagellation in the thirteenth century, which was highly approved by many holy men, [in which] the abuses were yet so frequent that Clement VI issued a bill against these processions."

The first recorded instances of sexual pleasure being obtained from flagellation, according to Ellis, surfaced in the late fifteenth century in the work *Disputationes Adversus Astrologiam Divinaricem* by Pico della Mirandola. Ellis also uncovered an account "of a man . . . who liked to be severely whipped, and found this a stimulant to coitus" written by one Coelius Rhodiginus in 1516. And in the *Onomasticon* of Otto Brunfels, written in 1534, Ellis found an article entitled "Coitus," which refers to the "case of a man who could not have intercourse with his wife until he had been whipped" (1942, 132).

"In 1643," Ellis reports, "Meibonius wrote *De Usu Flagorum in re Venerea*, the earliest treatise on this subject, narrating various cases" (1942, 132). Ellis also mentions a work by Schurig in 1720, *Spermatologia*, which describes many cases of people engaging in flagellation for pleasure. *Spermatologia* also reports an interesting variation of flagellation: urtication. The *OED* defines *urtication* as flogging "with fresh stinging-nettles" and further states that some forms of urtication were practiced for their medicinal values. (Apparently the crushing of certain types of stinging-nettles against the skin of people released disease-curing medicines into the bloodstream.) Finally, Ellis reports a letter that he discovered in his research from Nesterus to Garmann written in 1672 as the "earliest definitely described case of sadistic pleasure in the sight of active whipping which I have myself come across." The incident reported in the letter concerns an unnamed man "who, whenever in a school or elsewhere he sees a boy unbreeched and birched, and hears him crying out, at once emits semen copiously without any erection, but with great mental commotion" (1942, 132).

Though Krafft-Ebing was more interested in the manifestations of sadism and masochism in his work *Psychopathia Sexualis*, he did attempt to explain both the historical roots and the psychological motivations of the people who practiced this kind of sexual activity. He suggests that sadomasochism may have been derived from the sects of religious flagellants that flourished "in the thirteenth and fifteenth centuries" (1965; 22).

In Krafft-Ebing's view, an understanding of the similarities between religious and sexual behavior was important to an understanding of sadomasochistic sexual activity. "Religion as well as sexual love is mystical and transcendental," and in both spheres of human behavior more is going on than can be encompassed by the stated aims of either religion—"the possession of an object that is absolutely ideal, and cannot be defined by experimental knowledge"—or sexual activity—which has as its function the "propagation of the species" (1965, 5). According to Krafft-Ebing, both religious love and sexual love "are metaphysical processes which give unlimited scope to imagination" (1965, 5).

He goes on to state that nature "draws alike upon these

two spheres of conception, now forcing one, then the other into stronger activity, which degenerates into acts of cruelty either actively exercised, or passively endured" (1965, 6). Krafft-Ebing ties sadomasochism to religion by the twin cords of perversion and role-playing. He sees no difference between the degeneration of sexual activity from its prime function in creating the future of a species and the degeneration of religions from the paths originally set out for them to new paths more suited to their age but not intended by the religions' founders. Krafft-Ebing also notes—though he does not dwell on the point—that in both religion and sadomasochism there is role-playing in which the participants strive toward an ideal while ignoring or avoiding the seamier aspects of their actions (1965, 6):

> In religious life these may assume the shape of self-sacrifice or self-destruction, prompted by the idea that the victim is necessary for the material sustenance of the deity. The sacrifice is brought as a sign of reverence or submission, as a tribute, as an atonement for sins committed, or as a price wherewith to purchase happiness. If, however, the offering consists in self-punishment—and that occurs in all religions!—it serves not only as a symbol of submission, or an equivalent in the exchange of present pain for future bliss, but everything that is thought to come from the deity, all that is done in obedience to divine mandates or to the honour of the Godhead, is felt directly as pleasure. . . . Exaggerated religious enthusiasm also finds pleasure in the sacrifice of another person, when rapture combines with sympathy. *Similar manifestations may be observed in sexual life* [emphasis added].

Krafft-Ebing is drawing a direct correlation between the ideas and attitudes of religions toward self-sacrifice as a way to achieve pleasure and the attitudes of sadomasochists who seek to give or receive pain as a path to sexual satisfaction. He is very explicit here: just as religions have developed their ideas of self-sacrifice, self-punishment, and atonement by a victim for the sins of the faithful, so too have sadomasochists developed their ideas that sexual bliss can be found in physical and mental suffering.

Krafft-Ebing also draws on the tradition of romantic love as an explanation for sexual behaviors, including sadomasochism (1965; 7):

> First love always looks in a romantic idealizing direction. It wraps the beloved object in the halo of perfection. . . . To this may easily be traced many cases of misalliance, abduction, elopement and errors of early youth, and those sad tragedies of passionate love that are in conflict with the principles of morality or social standing, and often terminate in murder, self-destruction, and double suicide.

Transplanted into scenarios of sadomasochism, these acts of abduction and self-destruction become the very foundation of the sadomasochistic relationship. In fact, Krafft-Ebing goes on to say that "sentimental love is likely to degenerate into a burlesque," and he mentions the Knight of Joggengurg and Don Quixote as examples of the sentimental love of which he speaks. Both of these stories are also examples of courtly or romantic love, and could serve as role models for the sadomasochistic scenario.

While Krafft-Ebing goes on to suggest that women lack a sexual drive equal either in intensity or duration to that which men possess—a position no longer considered valid by students of human behavior—he unwittingly depicts another type of sadomasochistic scenario in his description of the overall effect of male-female sexual relationships (1965, 9 [emphasis added]): "In the sexual demands of man's nature will be found the motives of his weakness towards woman. *He is enslaved by her*, and becomes more and more dependent upon her as he grows weaker, and the more he yields to sensuality." This idea of woman as the dominant sexual partner and man as the submissive is crucial to the whole area of the professional dominatrix in sadomasochism. And the entire concept of female domination seems to have its roots in courtly love, in which the emphasis—though supposedly platonic—was actually on the woman controlling both the tenor of the relationship and the behavior of the man who was her servant in love.

Krafft-Ebing believed that love is "by no means simply a mystery of souls." To him, love could be explained in terms of "physical and mental peculiarities by which the attracting power is qualified" (1965; 11). He called this attracting power, "fetichism" (1965; 11).[4] "The word fetich," Krafft-Ebing said,

> signifies an object, or parts or attributes of objects, which by virtue of association to sentiment, personality, or absorbing ideas, exert a charm (the Portuguese "fetisso") or at least produce a peculiar individual impression which is in no wise connected to the external appearance of the sign, symbol, or fetich.

He continued (1965, 11 [emphasis in original]):

> The individual valuation of the fetich extending even to unreasoning enthusiasm is called *fetichism*. This interesting psychological phenomenon may be explained by an empirical law of association, *i.e.*, the relation existing between the notion itself and the parts thereof which are essentially active in the production of pleasurable emotions. It is most commonly found in *religious* and *erotic* spheres. *Religious* fetichism finds its original motive in the delusion that its object, *i.e.*, the idol, is not a mere symbol, but possesses divine attributes, and ascribes to it peculiar wonder-working (relic) or protective (amulet) virtues.
>
> *Erotic* fetichism makes an idol of physical or mental qualities of a person or even merely of objects used by that person, etc., because they awaken mighty associations with the beloved person, thus originat-

ing strong emotions of sexual pleasure. Analogies with religious fetishism are always discernible; for, in the latter, the most insignificant objects (hair, nails, bones, etc.) become at times fetiches which produce feelings of delight and even ecstasy.

We have cited the above extensive passage because Krafft-Ebing set out not only to describe sexual psychology but to demonstrate that so-called aberrant sexual behavior does not really differ much from so-called normal behavior. He not only likens sexual love to abnormal fixation, but considers sexual fetishism to be no different from religious behavior exhibiting the same characteristics. Krafft-Ebing stops short of saying that religious fetishism leads to sexual fetishism, or vice versa, but he is quite explicit in stating that the two types of fetishism differ only in specific application and not in general principles.

Krafft-Ebing goes on to say that when a person loves the entirety of another person—body, soul, and mind—this love is a true love and not a fetish. On the other hand (1965, 13),

where the body of the beloved person is made the sole object of love, or if sexual pleasure only is sought without regard to the communion of soul and mind, true love does not exist. Neither is it found among the disciples of Plato, who love the soul only and despise sexual enjoyment. In the one case the body is the fetich, in the other the soul, and love is fetichism. Instances such as these represent simply transitions to pathological fetichism.

So, for Krafft-Ebing, true love can exist between people only when the love is for what he would call the whole person: body, mind, and soul. All other manifestations of love are merely manifestations of fetishism.

This entire discussion of love is important to an understanding of sadomasochism because the ways in which love is defined would seem to be almost as important as the ways in which love is manifested. For Krafft-Ebing to treat of *ab-*

normal sexual activity, which is the topic of *Psychopathia Sexualis*, he first had to define normal sexual activity; and even though Krafft-Ebing has been criticized for his sexist approach to sexual relations, we must nevertheless acknowledge that his attitude is, at the very least, representative of his culture and his times. We must further acknowledge that his attitudes, both about sex and about women, still exist and are still popular with the bulk of Western society. Certainly with respect to sadomasochism it remains true that such behavior is not acceptable to the society at large. The benefit we derive from Krafft-Ebing's approach is that he recognizes implicitly that the difference between what is socially acceptable and what may not be socially acceptable is a matter of degree, and, further, that very often the line between the two is extremely difficult to discern.

If both Havelock Ellis and Krafft-Ebing are correct in seeing a link between ecstatic religious experience and sadomasochistic sexual activity, Krafft-Ebing provides the philosophical rationale, while Ellis supplies the historical detail. We merely note that in the absence of historical information refuting the notion that sexual ecstasy and religious ecstasy are similar, we can apply to Ellis's Greek, Roman, Syrian, and Persian flagellation exercises the same ideas Krafft-Ebing applies to the Christian ecstatics.

Of the flagellation sects that flourished in the thirteenth and fifteenth centuries, Krafft-Ebing says this (1965, 22):

> They were accustomed to whip themselves, partly as atonement and partly to mortify the flesh (in accordance with the principle of chastity promulgated by the Church—*i.e.*, the emancipation of the soul from sensuality). These sects were at first favoured by the Church; but, since sensuality was only the more excited by flagellation, and this fact became apparent in unpleasant occurrences, the Church was finally compelled to oppose it.

He proceeds to recount two examples of female religious flagellants and the nature of their public activities, and follows with some examples of males who required flagellation as a stimulant to sexual intercourse. He then presents the perceived cultural predilection toward flagellation in Russia and Persia—for Russia he has an example supporting the idea that flagellation was a normal part of marital relations—and he concludes his brief survey of sadomasochism in history with a report from the Roman historian Juvenal of "the woman [who] had herself whipped and beaten by the followers of Pan" (1965, 24). The reader of Krafft-Ebing's work cannot help but conclude that pain as a stimulant to sexual activity is as old as the human race.

We have made the point that in reading what both Ellis and Krafft-Ebing have to say about the history of sadomasochism, it is difficult to avoid the conclusion that practices that would today be considered part of the sadomasochistic subculture have very deep roots in human history. We must acknowledge, however, that because of the circumspection of those writers whose work has survived the ages, or because the ideas had not yet been promulgated generally within those early cultures, or, finally, because public punishment was such a commonplace fact of human culture that it had no connotations with sexuality, there are not conclusive links between the modern sadomasochistic subculture with its own language and code of behavior and the ancient events recounted earlier. As Ellis puts it (1942, 133):

> While, however, the evidence regarding sexual flagellation is rare, until recent times whipping as a punishment was extremely common. It is even possible that its very prevalence, and the consequent familiarity with which it was regarded, were unfavorable to the development of any mysterious emotional state likely to act on the sexual sphere, except in markedly neurotic subjects.

In formulating their theories about sadomasochism—indeed, even in defining the terms—Ellis and Krafft-Ebing both turned to literature for the support they could not find in the historical record, and, in one sense, literature provides a virtual treasure house for the study of the roots of sado-masochism. As an example, consider the following excerpt from Edgar Allen Poe's only novel, *The Narrative of Arthur Gordon Pym of Nantucket* (1956, 257–58). The narrator is discussing how he came to be fascinated with the seafaring life; notice, however, what Pym is really fascinated by:

It is strange, too, that he [Augustus] most strongly enlisted my feeling in behalf of the life of a seaman, when he depicted his more terrible moments of suffering and despair. For the bright side of the painting I had a limited sympathy. My visions were of shipwreck and famine; of death or captivity among barbarian hordes; of a lifetime dragged out in sorrow and tears, upon some gray and desolate rock, in an ocean unapproachable and unknown. Such visions or desires—for they amounted to desires—are common, I have since been assured, to the whole numerous race of the melancholy among men.

Although Poe's narrator is talking about the fantasies of a young man for the freedom of the seas, his words sound remarkably like those a masochist might choose to explain his or her general outlook to sadomasochistic sexual activity. Poe's narrator dwells on the torturous, the deprivational, and the horrific; that he attributes these feelings to men of a melancholy nature could merely be a reflection of the tastes of a repressive era in which sadomasochistic sexual thoughts would have to be severely circumscribed and hidden from public view.

As a second example, consider Reverend Dimmesdale, the Puritan minister from Nathaniel Hawthorne's *The Scarlet Letter*. Unable to repent publicly for his sin of adultery, Dimmesdale begins a series of self-tortures—lengthy, strength-draining fasts; all-night, exhaustive vigils, often with bright lights shining into his eyes; and, of course, horrible bouts of self-flagellation (1960, 143):

> In Mr. Dimmesdale's secret closet, under lock and
> key, there was a bloody scourge. Oftentimes, the Prot-
> estant and Puritan divine had plied it on his own
> shoulders; laughing bitterly at himself the while, and
> smiting so much the more pitilessly, because of that
> bitter laugh.

Critics most often read these lines merely as repeated acts
of penance, and we have no evidence that can detract from
that interpretation. But Dimmesdale's beatings of himself—
especially when accompanied by "that bitter laugh" that gave
him the strength to smite himself "so much the more piti-
lessly"—are certainly suggestive of someone who inflicts and
endures pain for reasons other than contrition.

Earlier we mentioned the place of sadomasochism in Greek
and Roman legend and life. A study of English literary history
reveals that sadomasochistic themes are hardly restricted
either to an unusual mind, such as Poe's, or a decadent
mind, such as de Sade's. In 1603 or 1604 George Chapman,
a playwright—a contemporary of Shakespeare—presented
Bussy d'Ambois. This play may have been the first performed
in the English theater to depict graphic scenes of torture on
stage. In any case, records indicate that it was a very popular
play. In 1748, while in debtor's prison, the first part of John
Cleland's *Memoirs of a Woman of Pleasure*—more popularly
known as *Fanny Hill*—was published; in 1749, Part II was
published, and Cleland was released from prison. *Memoirs*
contains several sadomasochistic scenes, along with a reference to the Hellfire Club, a real social organization of Cleland's time, the members of which seem to have engaged in
sadomasochistic practices on a regular basis. Not only are
these scenes presented with all the detail used in modern
erotic literature, but they are presented as activities not unexpected in the setting either of a house of prostitution or
of a club like the Hellfire Club.

De Sade wrote *Justine* in 1787 and *Juliette* a few years
later. While it is from de Sade that Krafft-Ebing took *sadism*,
de Sade was certainly not the first to write of sadomasochism
in French. Peter Sabor, in his introduction to *Memoirs*, notes

that Cleland may have been familiar with *L'Ecole des filles*, which was translated into English in 1655 as *The School of Venus*. Sabor also mentions *Satyra Sotadica* (1660), written by Nicolas Chorier. Sabor says that both books reveal an "enthusiasm for all forms of sexual encounters: homosexuality, lesbianism, sodomy, flagellation, and many other sexual variations." Clearly, sexual sadomasochism has existed both in literature and in life—and in more places than just England—for a long time.

In 1869, *Venus in Furs* was published. Written by Leopold von Sacher-Masoch, *Venus in Furs* describes the relationship between a woman and a man in which the man places himself totally in the service of the woman he loves. Over one hundred years old, this novel still serves as the basic plot for modern stories of masochism in which a man is completely dominated by the woman he loves. The heroine's name is Wanda, and she dresses habitually in furs. Interestingly, Sacher-Masoch's wife's name also was Wanda, and Ellis reports that Sacher-Masoch had a relative, a countess, who wore furs and was a domineering woman (1942, 114). Both Krafft-Ebing and Havelock Ellis take some pains to point out that Sacher-Masoch was either a practicing masochist or harbored masochistic fantasies.

Ellis's summary of Sacher-Masoch's life also contains the earliest documented personal advertisement for wife-swapping we have encountered in our research. According to Ellis (1942, 118, citing Wanda Sacher-Masoch's autobiography), Leopold constantly desired his wife to be unfaithful to him; in fact, "he even put an advertisement in a newspaper to the effect that a young and beautiful woman desired to make the acquaintance of an energetic man." The ad was answered, and Leopold bundled his wife off to an appointment at a hotel with her prospective lover, but Wanda convinced the unknown man that *she* was not interested in adultery, and he escorted her home.

One of the major British poets of the nineteenth century, Algernon Charles Swinburne, both wrote about and practiced masochism. Swinburne was a product of the English private school in which caning, paddling, and spanking were the normal and accepted punishments for infringement of the rules. His biographer, Jean Overtun Fuller, has provided us with a possible understanding both of Swinburne's fascination with masochism and of the fascination such activities hold for modern masochists (1968; 25):

> Flagellation was to haunt his poetry, his novels and his letters; all his life he was to be drawn back to it, as it were, longingly. . . . A "swishing" was an occasion for heroism, since the ability to take it without 'singing' was the test of a boy's mettle. Although Algernon was to grow to five feet four and a half inches, his large head and great shock of hair made his body look puny. Because this laid him open to the charge of unmanliness, he needed, and by bad behavior provoked, occasion to show that he could take punishment. The opportunity was so much greater because the punishment of junior boys was public.

Of course, in modern literature references to sadomasochism abound. In *S-M: The Last Taboo* (1974), Gerald and Caroline Greene have collected over a dozen excerpts from works by such writers as Baudelaire, George Colman, Edith Cadivec, and Pauline Reage that depict sexual sadomasochism. Erica Jong, Samuel Beckett, and others have also incorporated sadomasochistic activity into their work. Literature reflects many things about the society in which it is produced, and one of the things that it reflects is current preoccupations. Sadomasochism seems to be one of those preoccupations.

Sadism and masochism were a very great part of the everyday life of England until first flogging and then capital punishment were outlawed in modern Britain. It was common to expose all manner of miscreants in the stocks of England— the same kind of punishment occurred in the United States during the colonial period—and those so exposed were subjected to both the verbal and the physical abuse of all passersby as they suffered their terms of confinement. Until very recent history, the British Navy routinely flogged its sailors, and keelhauling was the traditional punishment for mutineers.[5] Another method for punishing prostitutes in England was "carting": the victim was tied to the back of a cart and then whipped out of town by one and all along the path.

So common was some form of flagellation in England that throughout the world to this day spanking, caning, and whipping are called "the English vice" even though there is no evidence to suggest that they were ever exclusively English. At least one source attributes the term *English vice* to the poet Swinburne, whose predilection for flagellation has already been mentioned. Havelock Ellis (1942; 130–31) said that

> whatever the precise origin of sexual flagellation in Europe, there can be no doubt that it soon became extremely common, and so it remains at the present day. Those who possess a special knowledge of such matters declare that sexual flagellation is the most frequent of all sexual perversions in England.

The term *English* and all of its compound forms are listed in our glossary; they all remain in use by the sadomasochistic subculture to this day as code words for spanking activities.

But it is unfair, as we have already mentioned, to claim that corporal punishment is strictly an English vice. We have shown how sadomasochism is an activity engaged in or written about by people of diverse backgrounds and cultural origins: Sacher-Masoch was an Austrian, de Sade a Frenchman, Poe an American; Andreas Spengler's statistics were drawn from Germans, and Maria Marcus, of Scandinavian descent, has written an excellent book (*A Taste for Pain*, 1981) on her own awakening—both physical and intellectual—as a masochist and feminist.

Sexual sadomasochism is the shared exploration of the use of restraint and pain in a role-playing environment by persons consenting to be in that environment. Those members of the subculture who have consented to be interviewed have stated repeatedly that respect for the limits of a willing partner is vital to any sadomasochistic relationship. To that end, a versatile language has been developed by the sadomaso-

chistic community to allow interested parties to communicate both their interests and their limits to other interested
parties. It is this language that serves as the primary focus
of the rest of this book.

The Language of Sadomasochism

METHODS AND CRITERIA

Below is a glossary of approximately 800 terms currently in use among people who engage in some form of sadomasochism. Before presenting the glossary itself, however, a number of prefatory comments are necessary regarding our methods and procedures for the collection and presentation of the terms it contains.

First, and perhaps most important, is the question of how and where the terms were collected. After combing through all of the available secondary sociological and psychological literature on sadomasochism[1] and finding very little lexicographic material,[2] we moved to three much more fruitful primary sources—personal ads, publications produced explicitly for members of the subculture, and personal interviews. Each of the personal ads was written by one or more sadomasochists for the purpose of locating one or more suitable and willing partners, and appeared in daily newspapers (with heavily coded language), in adult bookstores (all of which seem to have a large bulletin board devoted entirely to advertisements for sexual contact), in gay and leather bars (that is, bars known for the gay or sadomasochistic sexual orientation of many of their patrons), in two particular restrooms located in Ohio State University's main library (these restrooms had evidently been chosen by certain members of the subculture as a kind of public forum for the exchange of messages, philosophies, and advertisements), and in a number of magazines and periodicals produced explicitly for members of the subculture[3] (many of which—though not, strictly speaking, "underground" publications—were printed for a select readership and could be found only in adult bookstores, but some of which, surprisingly, were found in local convenience and grocery stores). These magazines and periodicals, along with catalogues of "torture" equipment and some explicitly sadomasochistic novels, also served as our second primary source of sadomasochistic terminology, for in addition to personal ads they inevitably contain a wealth of editorial and philosophical columns, short stories, "true-experience" letters to the editors, and advertisements for videotapes and "torture" equipment. Our last source of terminology, personal interviews, was certainly the most interesting if not always the most productive: it included telephone conversations with two professional dominatrices (who talked to us only after prolonged pleadings and profuse promises that we were in no way connected with any crime-control organization, and who refused to give their real names under any circumstances); mail correspondence with Briar Rose, a lesbian sadomasochistic support group located in a suburb of Columbus, Ohio (which, while extremely helpful, was also extremely wary of our motives and intent); in-person interviews with the owners of a number of adult clubs and bookstores (all but one of whom were so suspicious of us that the "interviews" might more accurately be termed "monologues"); and telephone interviews with the vice squad of the Columbus Police Department (members of which were as interested in what we could tell them about the language of sadomasochism as we were in what they could tell us).

A second question, once the terms were collected and defined, was which of them to include under the rubric "the language of sadomasochism"—a task considerably more difficult than it may sound, and in at least two ways. First, what counts as *the* language of sadomasochism? Easy to rule in were terms such as *golden shower, fistfuck*, and *horizontal bra*—that is, terms clearly included in the language of sadomasochism and found nowhere else; similarly, terms not used by the subculture were easy to rule out. But difficulties arose when identical terms were discovered in both the subcultural and the nonsubcultural language—terms such as *handcuffs*, for example, or *whip*—and, as will become evident, the number of such terms is considerable. In general, we included these terms ("in general" because of course we do not list function words, auxiliaries, and the like; and because we did not include terms such as *S* 'single', *W* 'white', *M* 'male', and so forth, all of which are clearly part of the language of personal ads and appear in the language of sadomasochism only because sadomasochists use such ads as a primary vehicle of communication)—not so much because they needed defining, but because to represent the language of sadomasochism without them would be inaccurate and misleading.[4] Second, what counts as the language of *sadomasochism*—that is, how should sadomasochism be defined? Should it include pederasty? Should it include child abuse, or spousal beatings, or mistreatment of the aged? Should it include homosexual or bisexual activities if they would normally be regarded as sadomasochistic between heterosexuals? In searching for guidelines as answers to these and similar questions, we found it useful to follow the parameters already established by psychologists and sociologists working in the field of sadomasochism or sexual deviation in general: Sadomasochism occurs when two adults agree to allow it to occur within certain preset rules and boundaries, and can include both psychological and physical abuse, fetishes and fantasies, and role-playing, any or all of which may or may not culminate in sexual orgasm.

Finally, we must consider the question of how limiting a study such as this is when so many of the data are gathered in a single location, Columbus, Ohio (a location which, though it certainly has its share of sadomasochists, can by no means be said to be the sadomasochism capital of the United States). At the risk of inviting criticism on all methodological fronts, we are confident that the study is not limited at all—that, in effect, the data presented below can be called "the language of sadomasochism" for the entire country and not just one city, state, or geographic region. We believe this primarily for four reasons: first, the publications devoted to sadomasochism that we examined circulate nationally and carry letters and personal ads from people in all fifty states; second, as will become evident from some of the ads cited below, many sadomasochists, especially professionals, travel extensively—often just within a certain area, such as the Midwest, but often nationwide—to meet and have encounters with other members of the subculture; third, the professional dominatrices we interviewed staunchly supported the view that no regional or social variation existed within the subculture (it would, they said, make communication through personal ads too difficult);[5] and fourth, though still largely an underground subculture, sadomasochists seem gradually to be coming out of the closet and forming support groups, holding rallies, and even organizing national conventions (lesbian sadomasochists had such a convention in Washington, D.C., in the fall of 1987), all with the intent of fostering greater unity and homogeneity—which homogeneity, we suppose, will naturally extend into their language as well.

And so to the terms themselves. Each entry in the glossary is listed alphabetically, using the following format: the headword occurs in **boldface** type and is followed by at least one *italicized* part-of-speech label; then, in parentheses, we have provided an etymology, perhaps tracing the term to the *OED* (*Oxford English Dictionary*), to *W9* (*Webster's Ninth New Collegiate Dictionary*), to Rawson (Hugh Rawson, *A Dictionary of Euphemisms and Other Doubletalk*, 1981), to Spears (Richard A. Spears, *Slang and Euphemism*, 1981), or to a work listed by author and date of publication and found in the References section at the end of the book, but just as often merely offering a probable date of coinage (e.g., "mid–20th century"); this is followed by the definition or definitions, any derivative forms (e.g., forms ending in -ing or -er) and their definitions, and a citation illustrating an actual usage of the word (given in quotation marks and followed by a parenthetical reference to its source, among which only the abbreviations *CLBR*, *CBD*, and *GT* have been used, for *Catalog of Leather Bondage and Restraints*, *Catalogue of Bondage and Discipline*, and *Gay Times* respectively); and following the citation are any synonyms of the term, explanatory notes or notes of interest, and *see also* references to related terms. All internal cross-references (i.e., those given within definitions) are indicated with an asterisk (*).

LIST OF ABBREVIATIONS USED

Most of the abbreviations used in this work are probably well known to most readers; however, to avoid any potential confusion, we provide the following comprehensive list of glosses:

adj	adjective
adj phr	adjective phrase
adv	adverb
c.	circa
CBD	*Catalogue of Bondage and Discipline* (no date, no publisher listed)
CLBR	*Catalogue of Leather Bondage and Restraints* (no date, no publisher listed)
col.	column
etym.	etymology, etymological
GT	*Gay Times*

inter	interjection
n	noun
no.	number
n phr	noun phrase
n pl	noun plural
OED	*Oxford English Dictionary*
OSU	Ohio State University
p.	page
Rawson	Hugh Rawson, *A Dictionary of Euphemism and Other Doubletalk* (New York: Crown, 1981)
Spears	Richard A. Spears, *Slang and Euphemism* (New York: Jonathan David, 1981)
v	verb
vol.	volume
v phr	verb phrase
W9	*Webster's Ninth New Collegiate Dictionary*

Glossary

A   *n* (probably 20th century)   *See* amazon   "Need A for B/D, light S/M" (personal ad, restroom wall, bar, Columbus, Ohio, 2/10/87).

abuse   **1:** *n* (*OED* 1580, 'violation, defilement') Physical or psychological punishment* and/or humiliation.* **2:** *v* (*OED* 1553, 'violate, ravage, defile') Infliction of such punishment and/or humiliation   "I enjoy being tied up, spanked and sexually abused by dominant males" (*Bizarre Lifestyles* 1, no. 1: 46, personal ad).

amazon   **1:** *n* (*OED* 1758, 'very strong, tall, or masculine woman')   Tall and/or large woman, especially one who is a dominatrix*   "Would like to meet females of all sizes, amazons most welcome" (*Bizarre Lifestyles* 1, no. 1: 43, per-

sonal ad). *Also* A. **2:** (probably 20th century)   *See* dominatrix   " 'BLACK AMAZON DIARY': Mistress Victoria is
5′11″—Black Amazon allows us to enter into the pages of her
diary" (*Women in Command* no. 16: 20, videotape ad). *Also*
A, bitch goddess, discipliness, dominant bitch, dominatrix
bitch, female dominant, femdom, goddess, headmistress,
mastix, mistress, queen.

amputee fetish   *n phr* (probably 20th century) Irra-
tional preoccupation with people who have various missing
appendages or who fantasize about or play the role of someone who has various missing appendages   "I specialize in
all kinds of domination: discipline, golden showers, brown
showers, TV training, foot worship, B & D, S/M, spanking,
enema, castration, cat fighting and amputee fetish" (*Corporal* 10, no 3: 33, personal ad).

anal rape   *n phr* (probably 20th century)   Forced anal
penetration, usually in connection with the fantasy of rape
"Protracted rituals, erotic interrogation, humiliation, wax,
whipping and anal rape make her wanton and wild" (*B & D
Pleasures* no. 56: 23, personal ad).

anilingus   *n* (W9 1949)   Oral stimulation of the anal
area   "Usually more graphic language is used, like 'like
ass,' but sometimes people who want to attract real educated
types use *anilingus*, sure" (personal interview, "Lucinda,"
2/19/87).

animal sex   *n phr* (probably 20th century)   Bestiality*
and oral sex with animals   "Widowed white male, 51, looking for women to 35 into animal sex" (*Intimate* 1, no. 1: 51,
personal ad).

animal training   *n phr* (probably 20th century) Sadomasochistic scenario* in which the submissive* is made to
act like an animal, usually a dog or a horse   "Enjoy animal

training, swinging, B & D, some S & M" (*B & D Pleasures* no. 56: 29, personal ad). *See also* doggie, kennel discipline, pony slave.

anklecuffs   *n pl* (see etym. note at cuffs; probably 20th century)   Cuffs* made specifically to fit on the ankles; the anklecuffs may be chained together or separated by leg spreaders* (*CBD*, p. 5, ad for anklecuffs).

anus worship   *n phr* (probably 20th century)   Fetish* for another's anus; prolonged anilingus* and Greek*   "If you desire bondage, boot, shoe, anus worship, spanking or humiliation, send a recent photo and SASE" (*Bizarre Lifestyles* 1, no. 1: 53, personal ad).

armbinder   *n* (probably 20th century)   Device used in sadomasochistic relationships to bind the arms of the masochist*; the armbinder may be made of leather, rope, chain, or barbed wire, and usually binds the arms to the body, perhaps with the aid of a lacing stick* ("Exquisite Agony," videotape). *See also* legbinder.

around the world   *n phr* (probably 20th century)   Variety of sexual positions and techniques, usually in quick succession   "Very uninhibited straight bondage loving TV adores stringent bondage, delicious french, foot-figure worshipping, around the world, seeks lengthy and hot sweaty sessions with all uninhibited white women" (*SM Express* no. 24: 26, personal ad).

arts   *n pl* (Rawson lists *English arts* 'sadism and or masochism'; probably 20th century)   Various methods of stimulation, copulation, and sadomasochism, including French,* Greek,* Roman,* Irish,* and sometimes Spanish*   "Most of us are into all the arts, you know, but some women shy away from the Roman way" (personal interview, "Lucinda," 2/19/87). *Also* love arts. *See also* cultures.

ass grease   *n phr* (probably 20th century)   Semen, especially that ejaculated during a session of Greek*   "For

an endless supply of ass grease (no S and M, yes B and D),
call [phone number]" (personal ad, restroom wall, OSU main
library, 3/11/87).

ass plug   *n phr* (see etym. note at plug; probably 20th
century)   Device used in sadomasochistic relationships to
completely fill the anus of the masochist*; ass plugs—used
especially in the retention of enemas—are usually made of
wood or plastic, vary in length from two to at least twelve
inches, and may be attached to a strap that runs under the
buttocks and fastens to a belt worn around the waist (*CLBR*,
p. 4, ad for ass plugs). *Also* butt plug.

aunt   *n* (Spears early 17th century, 'prostitute, especially
an old prostitute'; Spears 20th century, 'madam of a brothel';
Spears 20th century, 'aged sodomist'; Spears 20th century,
'aged fellator'; probably 20th century)   Disciplinary role*
played by a female or crossdressing male in a sadomasochistic scenario.* See citation at niece.

B   *n* (probably 20th century)   *See* bondage   "Expert
in H.D., C.P., B., W.S., TV's welcome" (*Women in Command*
no. 16: 29, personal ad).

backgammon   *n* (*W9* 1645, 'board game'; probably 20th
century)   Greek,* especially done repeatedly and fu-
riously   "WANTED: young lady for backgammon, French
lessons, light SM" (personal ad, restroom wall, OSU main
library, 3/10/87). *Also* G, Gr, GR, Greek arts, Greek culture.

backgammon player   *n phr* (see etym. note at backgammon; probably 20th century)   Person who especially enjoys backgammon*   "Backgammon players need have no
experience, will train, but must be enthusiastic about the
game" (personal ad, restroom wall, OSU main library, 3/10/
87).

back parlor   *n phr* (probably 20th century)   Buttocks,
including and often restricted to the anus   "Are you an

amazon with a soft back parlor that needs a gentle man's touch?" (personal ad, restroom wall, bar, Columbus, Ohio, 3/19/87). *Also* back yard.

back yard   *n phr* (probably 20th century)   *See* back parlor   "My back yard needs a strong male tool, if you're into light B/D and Greek, give me a call" (personal ad, restroom wall, bar, Columbus, Ohio, 3/17/87).

bad boy   *n phr* (probably 20th century)   Male masochist having the fantasy of being treated like a little boy, especially one that misbehaves   "Spankings by Dad, 51, for bad boys, gay or straight" (*Corporal* 10, no. 3: 37, personal ad). *Also* naughty boy.

bald eagle   *n phr* (probably 20th century)   Male genitals shaved of all hair   " 'Expert in penis torture, bald eagles my specialty' might be one way you'd see it [*bald eagle*]" (personal interview, "Lucinda," 2/19/87).

ball collar   *n phr* (probably 20th century)   Device used in sadomasochistic relationships to induce pain in the masochist's testicles; the ball collar is usually made of leather and resembles a bracelet in that it is slipped over the testicles and tightened above them. (*CBD*, p. 5, ad for ball collars).

ball gag   *n phr* (probably 20th century)   Kind of gag,* one that resembles a testicle; the ball gag is usually made of plastic and is attached to a leather strap that fastens behind the head of the submissive* when the ball gag is in his or her mouth   "Crotch ropes, panty gags, handcuffs, ball gags, hobble skirts, collars and chains" (*SM Express* no. 24: 6, videotape ad).

ball restraint ring   *n phr* (probably 20th century) Device used in sadomasochistic relationships to induce pain in the masochist's* testicles; the ball restraint ring is a metal or leather ring that fits over the testicle and can be tightened to any degree wished. (*CBD*, p. 5, ad for ball restraint rings).

ball stretcher   *n phr* (probably 20th century)   Device used in sadomasochistic relationships to inflict pain on a male masochist's* testicles; ball stretchers assume a variety of different forms, but all have in common the characteristic of two loops, through each one of which a testicle is passed; then, when the loops are tightened and pulled in opposite directions, the scrotum is stretched and pain occurs (*CBD*, p. 2, ad for ball stretchers). *See also* ball stretcher with chain.

ball stretcher with chain   *n phr* (probably 20th century) Kind of ball stretcher,* one with a metal chain hanging off of each loop, which chains can be pulled to cause pain (*CBD*, p. 2, ad for ball stretchers with chains).

b & d   *n phr* (abbreviation for bondage and discipline, Spears mid–20th century)   *See* bondage and discipline "If b & d isn't your game, it should be! Call me and let me introduce you to the finer things of life!" (personal ad, restroom wall, bar, Columbus, Ohio, 3/2/87). *Also* B & D, b and d, B and D, bd, BD, b/d, B/D, B.D., Burgers and Dogs.

B & D   *n phr* (abbreviation for bondage and discipline, Spears mid–20th century)   *See* bondage and discipline "Very exotic and sexually motivated Mistress into all aspects of B & D/S & M from light to very heavy" (*B & D Pleasures* no. 56: 21, personal ad). *Also* b & d, b and d, B and D, bd, BD, b/d, B/D, B.D., Burgers and Dogs.

b and d   *n phr* (abbreviation for bondage and discipline, Spears mid–20th century)   *See* bondage and discipline   "Young, hung, and into b and d? Call Linda at [phone number] FAST!" (personal ad, adult bookstore, Columbus, Ohio, 4/4/87). *Also* b & d, B & D, B and D, bd, BD, b/d, B/D, B.D., Burgers and Dogs.

B and D   *n phr* (abbreviation for bondage and discipline, Spears mid–20th century)   *See* bondage and discipline   "I'm hot and wet, VERY built (38D–23–36), and looking for someone to share innocent B and D with" (personal ad, adult bookstore, Columbus, Ohio, 4/1/87). *Also* b & d, B & D, b and d, bd, BD, b/d, B/D, B.D., Burgers and Dogs.

basket   *n* (Spears mid–20th century, homosexual usage)   Male genitals   "Ladies, if you want the biggest basket in town to whip, torment, and fuck your asshole, silly, I'm your girl [*sic*]" (personal ad, bar, Columbus, Ohio, 3/12/87). *See also* basket crusher. The author of this ad may be a she-male,* which would explain the apparent contradiction.

basket crusher   *n phr* (see etym. note at basket; probably 20th century)   Device used in sadomasochistic relationships to induce pain in the male's basket*; basket crushers come in a variety of forms, but all have in common the characteristic that they are capable of exerting tremendous pressure on all sides of the genitals simultaneously (*CBD*, p. 4, ad for basket crushers).

bd   *n phr* (abbreviation for bondage and discipline, Spears mid–20th century)   *See* bondage and discipline   "Swinger needs a little bd to be completely satisfied" (personal ad, restroom wall, OSU main library, 3/20/87). *Also* b & d, B & D, b and d, B and D, BD, b/d, B/D, B.D., Burgers and Dogs.

BD   *n phr* (abbreviation for bondage and discipline, Spears mid–20th century)   *See* bondage and discipline   "If you're into BD, heavy SM, call me, I can help you reach nirvana" (personal ad, restroom wall, bar, Columbus, Ohio, 2/16/87). *Also* b & d, B & D, b and d, B and D, bd, b/d, B/D, B.D., Burgers and Dogs.

b/d   *n phr* (abbreviation for bondage and discipline, Spears mid–20th century)   *See* bondage and discipline   "b/d for rent, your place or mine" (personal ad, adult bookstore, Columbus, Ohio, 1/30/87). *Also* b & d, B & D, b and d, B and D, bd, BD, B/D, B.D., Burgers and Dogs.

B/D   *n phr* (abbreviation for bondage and discipline, Spears mid–20th century)   *See* bondage and discipline   "Attractive, slim slave, 35, seeks others into sex, exotic leather and rubber attire, B/D and slavery" (*Bizarre Lifestyles* 1, no. 1: 46, personal ad). *Also* b & d, B & D, b and d, B and D, bd, BD, b/d, B.D., Burgers and Dogs.

B.D.   *n phr* (abbreviation for bondage and discipline, Spears mid–20th century)   *See* bondage and discipline   "Spank me to a crisp, then torture me with any B.D. that suits you" (personal ad, restroom wall, bar, Columbus, Ohio, 2/10/87). *Also* b & d, B & D, b and d, B and D, bd, BD, b/d, B/D, Burgers and Dogs.

beat the brains out   *v phr* (probably 20th century) Perform Irish*   "Need someone to dominate me, beat my brains out, no whips or chains" (personal ad, restroom wall, OSU main library, 3/12/87).

beefsteak and onions   *n phr* (Schmidt [1984] glosses the phrase 'with regard to sexual activities, the works'; probably 20th century)   General, unreserved sadomasochistic activities   "It's pretty odd, but it [*beefsteak and onions*] means S and M, no holds barred" (personal interview, vice squad, Columbus Police Dept., 3/11/87). *See also* beefsteak, hold the onions.

beefsteak, hold the onions   *n phr* (see etym. note at beefsteak and onions; probably 20th century)   Reserved sadomasochistic activities   "That [*beefsteak, hold the onions*] refers to lighter stuff—no real pain, you know" (personal interview, vice squad, Columbus Police Dept., 3/11/87). *See also* beefsteak and onions.

belt   *n* (*OED* c. 1000)   Strip of leather, perhaps adorned with chains, studs, jewels, etc., which is worn around the waist and to which a number of other devices such as ass plugs* and English cock harnesses* may be fastened (*CLBR*, p. 2, ad for belts).

bestiality   *n* (*OED* 1611, 'unnatural connexion with a beast')   Sexual act involving at least one human and at least one nonhuman animal, usually a horse or dog, but sometimes a pig, chicken, cat, or other animal   "I'm into it all, including cultures you've never dreamt of, bestiality (bring your own or use mine!), BD, SM the works" (personal ad, restroom wall, bar, Columbus, Ohio, 1/22/87). *Also* animal sex.

bi   *n, adj* (Spears mid–20th century)   Bisexual   "We are both bi and seek a passive partner for our mutual pleasure and desires. We're into greek and light B & D" (*Bizarre Lifestyles* 1, no 1: 51, personal ad). *Bi* also frequently occurs as a hyphenated compound, as in "Kinky bi-couple, she's 23, he is 39; seeking couples, females, males and groups" (*Intimate* 1, no 1: 57, personal ad)   or   "Young, attractive couple is seeking Bi-female or Bi-male to join us in threesome" (*Intimate* 1, no 1: 55, personal ad). *Also* bisexual.

bib   *n* (*W9* 1580, 'piece of cloth or plastic tied under the chin to protect the clothes')   Traditional bib used in infantilism* to humiliate* and discipline* the submissive* (*CBD*, p. 7, ad for bibs).

birching   *n* (*OED* 1845)   Act of spanking or beating with a switch or branch, originally made of birch, but now made of almost any wood available   "I also punish girls tit clamps [*sic*], cunnies ringed, full birchings, strapped down" (*B & D Pleasures* no. 56: 26, personal ad).

bisexual   *adj* (*W9* 1824)   Quality of being sexually oriented toward both sexes   "Bisexual bitch looking for young stud" (personal ad, adult bookstore, Columbus, Ohio,

2/23/87)   n (Spears 19th century)   Person who is sexually oriented toward both sexes   "I'm a bisexual female looking to experiment with b/d, light S and M" (personal ad, restroom wall, bar, Columbus, Ohio, 3/3/87). *Also* bi.

bitch goddess   *n phr* (probably 20th century)   *See* dominatrix   "Bitch goddess seeks sincere devotees desirous of being trained by demanding and arrogant dominatrix" (*Bizarre Lifestyles* 1, no. 1: 54, personal ad). *Also* amazon (2), discipliness, dominant bitch, dominatrix bitch, female dominant, femdom, goddess, headmistress, mastix, mistress, queen.

black handkerchief   *n phr* (probably 20th century) Heavy* sadomasochistic activities   "Let me see your black handkerchief!" (personal ad, restroom wall, OSU main library, 3/17/87). The black handkerchief, when worn so that it is visible to the public in an S and M bar, is also a visual signal that the wearer is looking for a partner to share heavy S and M.

blackroom   *n* (probably 20th century)   Room used for scenarios,* which room is painted a flat black color as in   "Complete dungeon, blackroom, plenty of toys" (personal interview, Briar Rose, Women's S/M Support Group, 2/27/87).

blanket   *n* (probably 20th century)   Partner for sadomasochistic relationship   "French and Greek teacher has lost her blanket and needs a new one fast!" (personal ad, restroom wall, bar, Columbus, Ohio, 2/14/87).

blindfold   **1:** *v* (*OED* 1225, 'cover the eyes, as with a bandage')   In a sadomasochistic scenario,* bind the eyes of the submissive* with a cloth or other object so as to render the person blind. **2:** *n* (*OED* 1880, 'device used to cover the eyes so as to render a person blind')   Device used to cover the eyes of a submissive as described in sense 1 (*CBD*, p. 10, ad for blindfolds).

blue handkerchief   *n phr* (probably 20th century)
Oral and/or anal sadomasochistic activities   "Show me
your blue handkerchief and I'll show you my black one" (personal ad, restroom wall, bar, Columbus, Ohio, 3/7/87). The
blue handkerchief, when worn so that it is visible to the
public in an S and M bar, is a visual signal that the wearer
is looking for a partner to share oral and/or anal activities:
light blue denotes oral; dark blue denotes anal.

body functions   *n phr* (probably 20th century)   Golden
shower,* brown shower,* enema,* or any combination of
these. See citation at piss enema.

body jewelry   *n phr* (probably 20th century)
Sadomasochistic equipment that is small and is used to inflict
pain on various parts of the body, such as nipple clamps,*
cock rings,* etc. (*CBD*, p. 3, ad for body jewelry).

body service   *n phr* (probably 20th century)
Sadomasochistic activities involving any and all parts of the
body; the activities frequently center on licking, sucking,
and/or kissing of various body parts such as the feet and
anus   "Mistress with beautiful firm body & tight openings
wants SLAVE tongues for full body service" (*Mistress* 2, no.
5: 20, personal ad).

body slave   *n phr* (see etym. note at slave; probably 20th
century)   Submissive* who will service the body of his or
her master* in whatever way the master specifies
-ery   (probably 20th century)   Activity of being a body
slave as described in sense 1   "BODY SLAVE seeking new
master for total devotion—you name it, I can do it better
than you've ever had it done to you before!" (personal ad,
restroom wall, OSU main library, 1/19/87).

body wax   n phr (probably 20th century)   Feces   "I
command all willing slaves to write me—I will interview and
choose those worthy to share my lovely body wax; into ene-

mas?" (personal ad, restroom wall, bar, Columbus, Ohio, 1/29/87).

body   worship   *n   phr*   (probably   20th   century) Complete slavery* in bondage and discipline,* which slavery frequently centers on the licking, sucking, and/or kissing of the dominant's* body   "We're interested in meeting other couples and single females interested in female domination, body worship and humiliation" (*SM Express* no. 24: 10, personal ad).   *Worship* may occur in combination with individual parts of the body as well, as in *foot worship*, *penis worship*, etc.; or in isolation as either a noun or a verb, as in   "Dominatrix wants your total worship" and   "I command you to worship me!"; and has given rise to the relatively recent *worshipper*, as in   "Experienced worshipper ready to serve you."

bondage   *n* (*OED* 1597, 'condition of being bound or tied up')   Physical restraint of one person by another in a sadomasochistic relationship, as through binding, cuffing, etc., or through the use of stocks, pillories, cages, etc.   "Los Angeles couple, he enjoys spanking, bondage, dominant or submissive females and docile bi-males" (*Bizarre Lifestyles* 1, no 1: 39, personal ad). *Bondage* is used frequently in combination with *discipline*, as in bondage and discipline.* *Also* burgundy handkerchief.

bondage and discipline   *n phr* (Spears mid–20th century)   Sadomasochistic scenario in which one person assumes a dominant* or directorial role, the other a submissive* or slave* role; the bondage and discipline may be either psychological or physical, and may include verbal abuse and threats as well as physical torture and punishment; *bondage and discipline* also denotes a difference in degree from sadomasochism,* the former usually taken to mean a lighter or less intense version of the latter   "White female into bondage and discipline, no S and M, seeks submissive slut males willing to come into my bondage, become my sex slaves, satisfy my every whim and desire" (personal

ad, restroom wall, bar, Columbus, Ohio, 5/2/87). *Also*, b & d,
B & D, b and d, B and D, bd, BD, b/d, B/D, B.D., Burgers
and Dogs. *Bondage* and *discipline* may also be used singly,
as in   "Looking for female to hold my spirit in bondage"   and   "Can you survive my discipline?"; or in combination with a specific part of the body, as in titty bondage*
and titty discipline*; and *discipline* often appears as a verb
(*OED* c. 1300, 'scourge or flog'; *OED* 1382, 'subject to discipline'), as in   "I have the experience necessary to discipline you."

bondage table   *n phr* (probably 20th century)   Table
used in bondage and discipline* for the purpose of strapping
or tying the submissive* down (*CBD*, p. 10, ad for bondage
tables).

bonds of humiliation   *n phr* (probably 20th century)
Implements used for bondage and discipline* and humiliation,* which implements include abusive language, odd
clothing, ropes, gags, and fetters of all kinds   "That night
she slept in handcuffs and leg irons, which I made her lock
herself into. She awoke me the next morning with breakfast
in bed, still in her bonds of humiliation" (*Corporal* 10, no.
3: 14). Sometimes clipped to *bonds*.

Boston tea party   *n phr* (probably 20th century)   *See*
brown shower   "Quiet homemaker looking for someone to
share Boston tea parties" (personal ad, restroom wall, bar,
Columbus, Ohio, 2/19/87). *Also* BS, B/S, hot turds, scat.

bottom   *n* (probably 20th century)   *See* masochist
"Looking for bottom to stick his nose between my cheeks,
also for water sports and total domination" (personal ad,
restroom wall, bar, Columbus, Ohio, 3/21/87). *Also* M (2),
masochist, passive, right hip pocket, S (3), slave, sub,
submissive.

bracelet   *n* (*OED* 1816, 'fetter for the wrist')   Anything
worn solely on the wrist in a sadomasochistic relationship,

including a leather wristband with studs and small spikes, handcuffs or other wrist restraints, etc. (*CBD*, p. 3, ad for bracelets).

bracelet cockring   *n phr* (probably 20th century)   Kind of cockring,* one which usually is adjustable and may be adorned with special decorations such as charms (*CBD*, p. 4, ad for bracelet cockrings).

brand   *v* (*OED* c. 1400)   Burn with hot iron "Looking for new pony to brand and stuff with hot meat" (personal ad, restroom wall, bar, Columbus, Ohio, 3/12/ 87)   **-ing**   *n*   (*OED* 1440)   Activity described in sense 1   "MATURE MASTER, extremely cruel and loving, has opening for two total slaves. M/F—Must be totally submissive to all my desires. Piercing, Branding, Etc." (*SM Express* no. 24: 14, personal ad).

breast press   *n phr* (probably 20th century)   Device used in sadomasochistic relationships to induce pain in the breasts of the female masochist*; the breast press may assume a variety of forms, but all have in common the characteristic of two parallel bars separated and fastened by steel bolts at either end which, after the breasts have been passed through the parallel bars, can be tightened, thus mashing the breasts from above and below and causing pain. (*B & D Pleasures* no. 56: 29, ad for breast press).

breast torture   **1:** *n phr* (probably 20th century)   Any form of torture inflicted upon the breasts of the submissive,* which torture may include binding with ropes or chains, piercing of the nipples, use of the breast press,* application of mousetraps or other clamps to the nipples, etc.   **2:** *v phr* (probably 20th century)   Inflict torture of the type described in sense 1   "Dominant single white male 54 seeks submissive female, short or long term, marriage possible or live-in. Into bondage, humiliation, breast torture, spankings, public & other fantasies" (*SM Express* no. 24: 12, personal ad). *Also* nipple bondage, nipple breast bondage, nipple discipline, nipple restraint, nipple torture, nt, tit bondage, tit discipline, tit torture, titty bondage, titty discipline, titty torture, tt.

bridle   *n* (*OED* c. 1000)   Device used in equestrian,* which device is identical to a horse's bridle with the exception of being scaled down to human size (*CBD*, p. 8, ad for bridles).

brown shower   *n phr*   Sadomasochistic activity involving (usually human) excrement, most often with one person defecating on another, perhaps with the help of an enema   "I also want to receive golden and brown showers from females, while being Greeked by males" (*Intimate* 1, no. 1: 44, personal ad). *Also* Boston tea party, BS, B/S, hot turds, scat.

brown sugar   *n phr* (Spears 20th century)   Black person, usually a female, interested in sadomasochism   "Looking for brown sugar to play S/M games with, nothing too severe" (personal ad, restroom wall, bar, Columbus, Ohio, 1/26/87).

BS   *n phr* (probably 20th century)   *See* brown shower   "Desperately need BS, GS, B and D, S and M, to satisfy curiosity" (personal ad, restroom wall, OSU main library, 2/21/87). *Also* Boston tea party, B/S, hot turds, scat.

B/S   *n phr* (probably 20th century)   *See* brown sugar   "I've tried GS, now want to try B/S with EXPERIENCED partner as giver" (personal ad, restroom wall, bar, Columbus, Ohio, 4/2/87). *Also* Boston tea party, BS, hot turds, scat.

bugger   *v* (*OED* 1611)   Penetrate the anus with a buggerclaw,* penis, dildo,* or similar device   **-ery** *n* (*OED* 1330)   Penetration of the anus as described in sense 1   "Need someone to bugger my hot hole—TVs okay, no gays" (personal ad, restroom wall, bar, Columbus, Ohio, 1/29/87).

buggerclaw   *n*   (see etym. notes at bugger, buggery)   Device used in buggery,* which device may be slightly curved and have several small protrusions on its body and end   "I'm into forced Greek, but NO buggerclaws" (personal ad, restroom wall, OSU main library, 1/30/87).

bull bitch   *n phr* (probably 20th century)   *See* she-male (2)   "Genuine bull bitches are rare, but they're in super hot demand by the blue video industry" (personal interview, "Lady in Black," 3/18/87).

Bullwhip   **1:**   *n*   (*W9* 1852)   Whip, usually made of leather and ranging in length from fifteen to twenty-five feet, used in sadomasochism. **2:**   *v*   (probably late 19th century)   Whip a masochist* with the device described in sense 1   "The naughty maid is bullwhipped, breast tortured and forced to remain in bondage all night" (*Women in Command* no. 16: 23, videotape ad).

Burgers and Dogs   *n phr* (Spears cites bondage and discipline as mid–20th century; probably 20th century)   Bondage and discipline* (*Burgers and Dogs* is a code phrase some bars use to signal potential patrons that people interested in bondage and discipline frequent the establishment. The phrase typically occurs on a sign outside the bar, and in no way reflects any menu of edible items.) *Also* b & d, B & D, b and d, B and D, bd, BD, b/d, B/D, B.D. *See also* spaghetti and macaroni.

burgundy handkerchief   *n phr* (probably 20th century)   Bondage,* especially implying the status of bottom*   "Burgandy [*sic*] handkerchief for sale, experienced and willing to travel" (personal ad, restroom wall, bar, Columbus, Ohio, 3/15/87). The burgundy handkerchief, when worn so that it is visible to the public in an S and M bar, is a visual signal that the wearer is looking for a partner to share in various bondage activities.

butch   *adj* (Spears mid–20th century, 'masculine lesbian,' homosexual usage; probably 20th century) Pertaining to a masculine lesbian interested in sadomasochism   "Enjoy TVs, butch women, couples" (personal ad, adult bookstore, Columbus, Ohio, 2/22/87).

butt plug   *n phr* (probably 20th century)   *See* ass plug   (*CLBR*, p. 4, ad for butt plugs).

CA   *n phr* (see etym. note at corporal arts)   *See* corporal arts   "Discipline lovers, take note: I'm the mistress of all CA, BD, SM, and I command you to call me NOW" (personal ad, restroom wall, OSU main library, 2/19/87). *Also* C/A, C.A., CD, C/D, C.D., corporal discipline, corporal punishment, CP, C/P, C.P.

C/A   *n phr* (see etym. note at corporal arts)   *See* corporal arts   "B/D, C/A, S/M, call [phone number]" (personal ad, OSU main library, 2/19/87). *Also* CA, C.A., CD, C/D, C.D., corporal discipline, corporal punishment, CP, C/P, C.P.

C.A.   *n phr* (see etym. note at corporal arts)   *See* corporal arts   "See me NOW for the best C.A. in town—well versed in French, Greek, Roman, Irish, willing to try anything twice" (personal ad, restroom wall, bar, Columbus, Ohio, 3/18/87). *Also* CA, C/A, CD, C/D, C.D., corporal discipline, corporal punishment, CP, C/P, C.P.

cage   *n* (*OED* c. 1225)   Small box, often having bars for walls, used for the confinement of submissives* (*CBD*, p. 8, ad for cages).

C and B torture   *n phr* (probably 20th century)   *See* cock and ball torture   "My interests are humiliation, public exhibitionism, nipple torture, hot wax, bondage, C & B torture, G.S." (*SM Express* no. 24: 26, personal ad).

candle wax torture   *n phr* (probably 20th century) Practice in sadomasochism* whereby hot wax from a candle is dripped onto a person's body to produce pain from the heat without causing a burn (see *B & D Pleasures* no. 56: 9, picture; and Califia 1980, 130). *Also* hot wax, wax, wax torture. *See also* ice cube.

cane   1:   *n*   (*OED* 1590)   Stick of wood, usually long and slender, used for spanking, whipping, and beating in sadomasochism. **2:**   *v*   (*OED* 1667)   Whip or beat with implement as described in sense 1   ˉ "The young college boy is caned, cropped and soundly thrashed over the knee of this 52EE Bosom of Mistress Lotta, then thoroughly caned and paddled beneath the cold and wicked Dutchess von Stern!" (*Women in Command* no. 16: 7, videotape ad).

canine   interest(s)   *n phr* (probably 20th century) Interest in incorporating dogs into the sadomasochistic scenario*   "Young and wild, into everything, even canine interests" (personal ad, adult bookstore, Columbus, Ohio, 2/12/87). *See also* pets.

canned goods   *n pl* (Spears 20th century, 'male or female virgins'; probably 20th century)   Virgins to the sadomasochistic experience   "Now accepting slaves, no canned goods, please" (personal ad, restroom wall, bar, Columbus, Ohio, 2/14/87). Usually used derogatorily.

cannibal   *n phr* (Spears 20th century, 'homosexual male fellator'; probably 20th century)   One especially given to French* and anilingus*   **-ism**   *n*   (probably 20th century)   French and anilingus   "Cannibal, 29, male, well-built, would like to meet new 'victims' soon, also for light B & D, perhaps some S & M" (personal ad, restroom wall, OSU main library, 3/8/87).

captive   n (*OED* c. 1400, 'one taken and held in confinement')   In bondage,* the submissive,* especially one who is bound, gagged, or otherwise fettered so as to be made completely powerless   **-ity**   n   (OED 1325, 'state of being held in confinement')   Condition described in sense 1 "I never made any men my captives or anything; I was strictly doing light stuff" (personal interview, "Lucinda," 2/19/87).

castrate   **1:**   v   (*OED* 1633)   Sever; remove, especially the genitals. **2:**   n   (*OED* c. 1420)   See citation at amputee fetish. (According to Dr. Robert Birch [personal interview, 3/11/87], a sex therapist, *castration* refers only to the symbolic removal of the penis; however, cases have been cited in the medical literature in which overzealous sadists have committed nonsymbolic castration as well.)

cat   **1:**   n   (*OED* 1788)   Cat-o-nine-tails*   "My delights include: Leather, black lingerie, boots, paddles, cats and golden showers. Enemas to the faithful!" (*Bizarre Lifestyles* 1, no. 1; 48, personal ad). **2:**   v   (*OED* 1788)   Whip or flog, especially with the cat-o-nine tails   "Let me cat you, you'll never want it to end" (personal ad, adult bookstore, Columbus, Ohio, 3/13/87).   *Also* cat fighting (v).

cat-fighting   n phr   (see etym. note at cat; probably 19th–20th century)   Sadomasochistic activity in which two partners slash at each other with cats*   "Dominant seeks other dominant for wrestling, cat fighting, sharing of slaves" (personal ad, restroom wall, bar, Columbus, Ohio, 3/12/87). *Also* cat (v).

cat-o-nine-tails   n phr   (*OED* 1695)   Kind of whip* that has nine strands of leather (rather than only one) attached to its handle; each of the nine strands is usually knotted at the end, and may have a steel ball or stud as well   "No one can sling a cat-o-nine-tails like my dominant wife!" (personal ad, restroom wall, bar, Columbus, Ohio, 2/11/87). *Also* cat (n).

CD   *n phr* (see etym. note at corporal arts)   *See* corporal arts   As in "Have complete line of equipment for CD" (information supplied by vice squad, Columbus Police Dept., 3/11/87). *CD* is an abbreviation of corporal discipline. *Also* CA, C/A, C.A., C/D, C.D., corporal discipline, corporal punishment, CP, C/P, C.P.

C/D   *n phr*   (see etym. note at corporal arts)   *See* corporal arts   As in "Cum enjoy torturous C/D in my chambers" (information provided by vice squad, Columbus Police Dept., 3/11/87). *C/D* is an abbreviation of corporal discipline. *Also* CA, C/A, C.A., CD, C.D., corporal arts, corporal discipline, corporal punishment, CP, C/P, C.P.

C.D.   *n phr*   (see etym. note at corporal arts)   *See* corporal arts   As in "B.D. and C.A., no S.M., this mistress" (information provided by vice squad, Columbus Police Dept. 3/11/87). *C.D.* is an abbreviation of corporal discipline. *Also* CA, C/A, C.A., CD,C/D, corporal discipline, corporal punishment, CP, C/P, C.P.

chain   1:   *n*   (*OED* c. 1300)   Connected, flexible series of links, usually made of metal, used for binding submissives*   in   sadomasochistic   relationships. **2:**   *v*   (*OED* 1393)   Bind with a chain such as that described in sense 1. See citation at ball gag.

champagne   *n*   (probably 20th century)   Urine, especially that from a golden shower*   "Come drink at my fountain, drink my champagne" (personal ad, adult bookstore, Columbus, Ohio, 3/30/87).

chastity harness   *n phr*   (*W9* 1931, *chastity belt*; probably 20th century)   Device that may be used in sadomasochistic relationships and worn by women; the device usually ties or buckles around the waist and consists of a piece of triangular leather—which may be variously adorned with studs, small chains, etc.—that covers the pudendum and has a slit or screen to allow urination but will not allow oral or sexual intercourse (*CLBR*, p. 6, ad for chastity harnesses).

cheek bite **1:** *n* (Spears 18th century, *cheeks* 'buttocks'; probably 20th century)   Biting of a sadomasochistic partner's buttock, perhaps to the point of drawing blood. **2:** *v* (probably 20th century)   Bite as described in sense 1   "Into welts, blood, cheek biting?" (personal ad, restroom wall, bar, Columbus, Ohio, 3/15/87).

cherry-stuff *v* (Spears 20th century, *cherry* 'hymen'; probably 20th century)   Place foreign objects into a sadomasochistic partner's vagina; the foreign objects can be parts of the other partner's body, but usually include dildos and a wide variety of other objects   **-ing** *n* (probably 20th century)   Procedure described in sense 1   "Female, 21, well-endowed, 38–22–35, needs male master for humiliation, bondage, cherry-stuffing" (personal ad, restroom wall, OSU main library, 1/22/87).

clamp **1:** *n* (*OED* 1688)   Device used to compress some part of a person's body in a sadomasochistic scenario,* as in a nipple clamp.* **2:** *v* (*OED* 1677–96)   Use a clamp as described in sense 1   (*CBD*, p. 3, ad for clamps). *See also* clip.

clean *adj* (*OED* 883, 'undefiled, unsullied')   Free of disease   "Young, bi-girl interested in meeting women and couples w/bi-wives for unusual adventures. Can travel. Must be clean" (*Bizarre Lifestyles* 1, no. 1: 41, personal ad).

clip **1:** *n* (*OED* 1470)   Device used to clasp or pinch a part of the body of a sadomasochist. **2:** *v* (*OED* c. 1000)   Clasp a part of the body as described in sense 1   (*CBD*, p. 3, ad for clips). Clips differ from clamps* in that the former are usually lighter and inflict less pain than the latter. Both are most frequently used on the nipples, clitoris, penis, and testicles. *See also* clamp.

closed swinging   *n phr* (probably 20th century)
Swinging* limited usually to one couple or threesome and
done with no spectators or cameras and in the privacy of
one's own bedroom or dungeon*   "Partner(s) wanted for
light S and M, closed swinging" (personal ad, restroom wall,
bar, Columbus, Ohio, 2/16/87).

clothes pin torture   *n phr* (probably 20th century)   Form of torture* in which clothes pins are clamped
on to various parts of the body, often the penis and testicles
or, most frequently, the breasts and especially the nipples   "Amy was familiar with clothes pin torture, in fact
she had once won a $100 bet for her Master by being able
to withstand a whole package of fifty pins being clamped to
her body and through her labia, nipples and the fleshy mounds
of her buttocks, pubes and breasts had stung for days af-
terward [*sic*], the look of pride on her Master's face as she
stood on the pool table in the bar at Red Rock Arizona bris-
tling with clothes pins like a porcupine had been worth the
pain" (*B & D Pleasures* no. 56: 15, cols 2–3).

cock and ball harness   *n phr* (probably 20th century)   Device that may be used in sadomasochistic relationships, which device consists of two collars made of
leather (usually adjustable, and often decorated with studs)
and joined by a third strip of leather; one collar fits around
the testicles and base of the penis, the other around the
middle or the tip of the penis (*CLBR*, p. 5, ad for cock and
ball harnesses).

cock and ball torture   *n phr* (probably 20th century)   Sadomasochism involving torture* to the penis and
testicles, which torture may include constriction, stretching,
crushing, piercing, etc.   "Ice breaker at swingers' parties—suck feet, cocks, cunts, serve drinks and happily endure extreme self or female inflicted cock and ball torture"
(*Intimate* 1, no. 1: 38, personal ad). *Also* C & B torture.

cockblock   1:   *v*   (Spears mid–20th century. Black
usage, *cockblock* 'interfere with a man's sexual activity with

a woman; probably 20th century)   Bind the penis, as with nylon stocking, in such a way that the binding can be tightened quickly to prevent ejaculation. **2:**   *n*   (probably 20th century)   Activity described in sense 1. **3:**   *n*   (probably 20th century)   Stocking or other material used as described in sense 1   **-er**   (probably 20th century)   Person doing the activity described in sense 1   **-ing**   (probably 20th century)   Activity described in sense 1   Repeated cockblocking causes extreme pain, especially in the testicles, and is a favorite method of cock and ball torture.*   "Experienced dominatrix specializes in training male slaves with cockblocking" (personal ad, restroom wall, bar, Columbus, Ohio, 2/19/87).

cock harness   *n phr* (probably 20th century)   *See* English cock harness (*CBD*, p. 5, ad for cock harnesses).

cock mouth gag   *n phr* (probably 20th century)   Gag* consisting of an adjustable leather strap with a rubber or plastic penis protruding from the middle of it; the strap is tied around the submissive's* head and the penis placed in his or her mouth as a means of discipline* and restraint* (*CLBR*, p. 5, ad for cock mouth gags). *Also* dick gag. *See also* plug gag.

cockring   *n* (probably 20th century)   Ring, usually made of steel or some other hard metal, large enough to slip onto a limp penis; when the penis then becomes erect, the ring serves both to induce a great deal of pain and to trap blood within the penis, thus sustaining the erection for a longer period of time (*CLBR*, p. 4, ads for cockrings). Sometimes occurs as two words; *also* CR, C/R, C.R. *See also* studded cockring.

cockwhip   **1:**   *n* (see etym. note at whip; probably 20th century)   Small whip* made especially for flagellation of the penis. **2:**   *v*   (probably 20th century)   Flagellate as

described in sense 1   **-ing**   (probably 20th century)
Flagellation as described in sense 1   (*B & D Pleasures*,
no. 56: 29, ad for cockwhips).

collar   *n* (*OED* 1337)   Piece of adjustable chain or
leather that is usually put around the submissive's* neck as
a means of discipline* and bondage*; the collar may serve as
part of a scenario* in which the submissive is made to act
and behave like a dog (*CLBR*, p. 2, ad for collars).

corncob   *n* (probably 20th century)   Kind of dildo,* one
with small spikes of hard rubber or plastic protruding from
the sides (*CBD*, p. 5, ad for corncobs).

corporal arts   *n phr* (*OED* lists *corporal* (adj) 'physical
punishment', c. 1400; probably 20th century)   Sadism,*
including all forms of punishment and torture, both verbal
and physical   "B&D, S&M, TV, corporal arts, fetish orientation of leather boots, feet, heels, corsetry, etc." (*Women
in Command* no. 16: 29, personal ad). *Also* CA, C/A, C.A.,
CD, C/D, C.D., corporal discipline, corporal punishment, CP,
C/P, C.P.

corporal discipline   *n phr* (see etym. note at corporal
arts)   *See* corporal arts   "She is further taught to walk,
talk and act more lady like through Corporal Discipline"
(*Women in Command* no. 16: 29, video ad). *Also* CA, C/A,
C.A., CD, C/D, C.D., corporal punishment, CP, C/P, C.P.

corporalist   *n* (see etym. note at corporal; probably 20th
century)   Sadist*   "Refined corporalist commands you
to phone him!" (personal ad, restroom wall, bar, Columbus,
Ohio, 2/16/87). *Also* dom, dominant, left hip pocket, M (3),
master, S (2), sender, sir, taskmaster, top.

corporal punishment   *n phr*   *See* corporal arts   "A
lot more people are into the whole corporal punishment scene
than you'd probably guess" (personal interview, "Lucinda,"
2/19/87). *Also* CA, C/A, C.A., CD, C/D, C.D., corporal discipline, CP, C/P, C.P.

correction   *n* (*OED* 1386)   Discipline*; dominance*
"Training, discipline and correction will be provided" (*B &
D Pleasures* no. 56: 23, personal ad).

corset   *n* (*OED* 1299, *corset* in the traditional
sense)   Anything resembling a traditional corset used to
bind the body, including plastic wrap, sheets, deflated inner
tubes, etc. **-ry**   *n* (probably 20th century)
Binding of the body in a corset or corsets; the binding frequently occurs around parts of the body other than the traditional abdominal and trunk regions and is usually
intended to render the bound person powerless. See citation
for corporal arts.   "You get a lotta guys, they want to be
trussed up in corsets, I think because it makes them feel
completely at the mercy of the dominatrix" (personal interview, "Lucinda," 3/2/87).

couple   *n* (*OED* 1759)   Two people, most often a man
and woman, both of whom practice some form of sadomasochism   "I'll travel anywhere, all expenses paid by the
guy, gal or couple" (*Bizarre Lifestyles* 1, no. 1: 47, personal
ad). *Also* cpl.

CP   *n phr* (probably 20th century)   Corporal arts*
"BD, CP, SM, all kinds" (personal ad, restroom wall, Larry's
Bar, Columbus, Ohio, 4/2/87). *CP* is an abbreviation of corporal punishment. *Also* CA, C/A, C.A., CD, C/D, C.D., corporal discipline, corporal punishment, C/P, C.P.

C/P   *n phr* (probably 20th century)   Corporal arts*
As in "C/P, no heavy S/M" (information provided by vice
squad, Columbus Police Dept., 3/5/87). *C/P* is an abbreviation of corporal punishment. *Also* CA, C/A, C.A., CD, C/D,
C.D., corporal arts, corporal discipline, corporal punishment, CP, C.P.

C.P.   *n phr* (probably 20th century)   Corporal arts
See citation at C/P. C.P. is an abbreviation of corporal pun-

ishment. *Also* CA, C/A, C.A., CD, C/D, C.D., corporal discipline, corporal punishment, CP, C/P.

cpl.   *n* (see etym. note at couple; probably 20th century)   *See* couple   "Attractive Bi-couple, mid 30's, seeking Bisexual cpls., Single Bi-females and males, 21 to 40" (*Intimate* 1, no. 1: 52, personal ad).

CR   *n* (probably 20th century)   *See* cockring   As in "We carry the largest selection of CR's you'll find anywhere" (information provided by the vice squad, Columbus Police Dept., 3/27/87). *Also* C/R, C.R.

C/R   *n* (probably 20th century)   *See* cockring.   (*The Underground*, ads for cockrings). *Also* CR, C.R.

C.R.   *n* (probably 20th century)   *See* cockring   As in "Customized C.R.'s, any size, allow six weeks delivery time" (information provided by vice squad, Columbus Police Dept., 3/27/87). *Also* CR, C/R.

crop   **1:**   *n*   (*OED* 1857)   Riding crop, which is frequently used in the whipping of masochists.*   **2:**   *v*   (probably 20th century)   Whip with a riding crop   "Sherman Sothern grunted in sadistic pleasure, and began to slice the crop back and forth across Pruett's buns, uttering hoarse, obscene things beneath his breath" (*Expose!*, p. 26).

cross   **1:**   *v*   (probably 20th century)   Crossdress.*   **2:**   *n*   (*OED* c. 1300)   Device used in sadomasochism, which device consists of two poles or boards joined at their approximate centers and at right angles to one another, and to which the submissive is lashed or chained to render him or her immobile   (*CBD*, p. 8, ad for crosses)   **-ing**   *n*   (probably 20th century) *See* crossdress   "Stockings, garters, high heels, B & D fantasies in my private dungeon!! P.S. Crossing too!" (*Women in Command* no. 16: 26, personal ad).

crossdress *v* (probably 20th century)   Practice transvestism in public, usually of a man   **-er** *n*   (probably 20th century)   Practice of transvestism in public, usually by a man   "Dominant: 30, woman into leather seeks sissy men only who are either crossdressers, transvestites, or shemales" (*Intimate* 1, no 1: 58, personal ad)   **-ing** "Crossdressing is my special fantasy" (personal ad, adult bookstore, Columbus, Ohio, 2/12/87). *Also* cross *(v). See also* transvestite. The differences between standard transvestism and crossdressing lie in the former usually being private and self-motivated and the latter being public and disciplinary (i.e., part of a scenario*).

crotch rope *n phr* (probably 20th century)   Kind of rope used in sadomasochistic relationships, which rope is usually made of a soft material such as velvet and used to tie the more sensitive parts of the body such as the (usually female) crotch (See citation at ball gag.) *Also* velvet rope.

cuffs *n pl* (*OED* 1663)   Metal or steel rings that are typically placed around the submissive's* ankles or wrists; the rings are usually joined together by a chain or steel bar of varying length (*CBD*, p. 7, ad for cuffs). *See also* anklecuffs, handcuffs.

cultured *adj* (probably 20th century)   Experienced in some, and usually all, of the various cultures*   "Cultured girl seeks novice for enthusiastic tutoring" (personal ad, adult bookstore, Columbus, Ohio, 4/11/87).

cultures *n pl* (probably 20th century)   Any combination of English,* French,* Greek,* Irish,* Roman,* and Spanish*   "Dominatrix experienced in all cultures and fantasies now accepting applications for new slaves" (personal ad, adult bookstore, Columbus, Ohio, 2/18/87). *See also* arts.

cum freak *n phr* (Spears mid–20th century, 'young woman interested only in copulating'; probably 20th century)   Person who seemingly thrives on semen, especially its ingestion   "Petite, 105 lbs., shaved cunt, erect nipples is a cum freak. . . . Swallows cum loads pumped into her. Licks cum from cunts. . . . Swallows all cum pumped into her and on her" (*Bizarre Lifestyles* 1, no. 1: 56, personal ad).

cum queen   *n phr* (Spears 20th century or before, *cum* 'semen'; Spears mid–20th century, *queen* 'male homosexual'; probably 20th century)   Female or gay male cum freak*   "Cum queen (female) looking for ample supply of milk" (personal ad, restroom wall, OSU main library, 2/11/87).

dark blue handkerchief   *n phr* (probably 20th century) Sadomasochist who prefers anal to oral activities   "Need dark blue handkerchief for forced Greek" (personal ad, adult bookstore, Columbus, Ohio, 2/26/87). The dark blue handkerchief, when worn so that it is visible to the public in an S and M bar, is a visual signal that the wearer is looking for a partner to share anal activities.

devote   *v* (*OED* 1604, 'swear allegiance to'; probably 20th century)   Be definitely interested in sadomasochism in some form, as opposed to having only a mild* interest **-ed**   *adj*   (*OED* 1600, 'having complete allegiance to'; probably 20th century)   One with an interest in sadomasochism as described in sense 1   **-ee**   *n*   (*OED* 1657–83, 'one who has complete allegiance to'; probably 20th century)   One with an interest in sadomasochism as described in sense 1   **-ion**   *n*   (*OED* c. 1530, 'complete allegiance'; probably 20th century)   Interest in sadomasochism as described in sense 1   See citation at bitch goddess.

DHB   *n phr* (see etym. notes at discipline, humiliation, and bondage; probably 20th century)   Discipline,* humiliation,* and bondage*   "Looking for serious DHB play-

mate" (personal ad, adult bookstore, Columbus, Ohio, 1/28/
87). *Also* D.H.B., D/H/B.

D/H/B   *n phr* (see etym. note at DHB; probably 20th century)   *See* DHB   "Slave looking for D/H/B master" (personal ad, restroom wall, bar, Columbus, Ohio, 3/22/87). *Also*
D.H.B.

D.H.B.   *n phr* (see etym. note at DHB; probably 20th century)   *See* DHB   "WANTED: Water sports enthusiast to
teach the arts of D.H.B. to willing and eager learner" (personal ad, restroom wall, bar, Columbus, Ohio, 2/15/87). *Also*
D/H/B.

dick gag   *n phr* (probably 20th century)   *See* cock
mouth gag   (*CBD*, p. 5, ad for dick gags).

dildo   *n* (*OED* 1610)   Artificial penis; anything used as
a penis in sexual intercourse or Greek*   "Female slave,
young and BUILT, looking for 10–12″ cock or dildo for forced
Greek" (personal ad, restroom, Ohio State University main
library, 2/28/87).

discipline   **1:**   *n*   (see etym. note at B & D; *OED*
1659, 'system of rules for conduct'; *OED* c.1450, 'order maintained and observed among persons under control'; *OED*
1225, 'correction, punishment inflicted'; *OED* 1622, n, 'instrument of chastisement')   Sadomasochistic scenario*
in which one person dominates another, usually through
physical punishment* such as spanking,* bondage,* etc., as
well as through oral abuse* and all types of humiliation.*
2:   *v*   (see etym. note at B & D; *OED* 1382, 'subject to
discipline'; *OED*, c. 1300, 'scourge or flog')   Administer discipline of the sort described in sense 1   "You need my
discipline, you slut slave! Let me grind my shit into you,
worthless cumbag!" (personal ad, restroom wall, bar, Columbus, Ohio, 3/18/87). Frequently used in combination with
bondage and humiliation; *also* b & d, B & D, b and d, B and

D, bd, BD, b/d, B/D, B.D., bondage and discipline, Burgers and Dogs, H/D, H.D.

discipliness   n (probably 20th century)   See dominatrix   "Experienced discipliness can make you obey her every need!" (personal ad, restroom wall, bar, Columbus, Ohio, 3/9/87). Also amazon (2), bitch goddess, dominant bitch, dominatrix bitch, female dominant, femdom, goddess, headmistress, mastix, mistress, queen.

disobedient   adj (OED c. 15th century, 'not obedient')   In a sadomasochistic scenario,* the slave* not obeying* every whim of the master   **-ence**   n   (OED c. 1400, 'action or state of not being obedient')   Disobedient behavior of the sort described in sense 1   "Premier mistress demands you slut slaves to contact her! I do not tolerate disobedience, I am not for the faint hearted!" (personal ad, adult bookstore, Columbus, Ohio, 1/19/87).

docile   **1:**   n   (probably 20th century)   Person who gains sexual satisfaction from being bound, gagged, beaten, disciplined,* or humiliated.*   **2:**   adj   (OED 1774, 'tractable'; probably 20th century)   Exhibiting behavior described in sense 1   "Young white docile needs to be enslaved by your hot, moist cunt" (personal ad, restroom wall, OSU main library, 3/19/87).

doggie   **1:**   n   (Spears, dog-fashion 'anal copulation on a woman'; 20th century or before; probably 20th century)   Kind of humiliation,* one in which one person makes the other perform or act like a dog.   **2:**   adj   (probably 20th century)   Exhibiting behavior described in sense 1   "Slave needs master for doggie" (personal ad, restroom wall, bar, Columbus, Ohio, 3/12/87); "I wore a black leather g-string, . . . a studded dog collar and leash, and suspenders attached to the g-string serving as a sort of harness. . . . She led me around on all fours by the leash around my neck . . . she made me bark like a dog, begging for cookies she fed me from gloved hands" (*Corporal* 10, no. 3: 6, 9). *Also* kennel discipline, kennel training.

dom   *n* (see etym. note at dominant; probably 20th century)   *See* sadist.   See citation at dominant.   *Also* dominant   *dom* is an abbreviation of dominant. *Also* corporalist, left hip pocket, M (3), master, S (2), sender, sir, taskmaster, top.

dominant   1:   *n*   (*OED* 1532, 'one who controls'; probably 20th century)   *See* sadist   *Also* corporalist, dom, left hip pocket, M (3), master, S (2), sender, sir, taskmaster, top. **2:**   *adj.* (probably 20th century)   Sadistic; domineering,   in   a   sadomasochistic   scenario* **-ance**   (*OED* 1819, 'state of controlling or being controlled')   *Also*   correction,   discipline   **-ate** *v*   (*OED* 1611, 'master')   In a sadomasochistic relationship, control the actions of another   "Couple, he dominant, white, tall, slim, 30's. She submissive, black, slender, 22, seek females, Dom or Sub, Gay or Straight, for interesting meetings" (*Women in Command* no. 16: 28, personal ad).

dominant bitch   *n phr (see etym. note at* dominant; probably 20th century)   *See* dominatrix   "Dominant Italian Bitch wants to hear from all submissives willing to serve me, as My slave"   (*Women in Command* no. 16: 25, personal ad). *Also* amazon (2), bitch goddess, discipliness, dominatrix bitch, female dominant, femdom, goddess, headmistress, mastix, mistress, queen.

dominatrix   *n* (*OED* 1561, 'female dominator')   Female sadist, especially one with a male masochist for a partner; woman   who   dominates   a   sadomasochistic   relationship   "Ruby rose haired, hazel eyed, attractive, popular, experienced dominatrix 36 years [*sic*], leads male novices into erotic world" (*Bizarre Lifestyles* 1, no. 1: 52, personal ad). *Also* amazon (2), bitch goddess, discipliness, dominant bitch, dominatrix bitch, female dominant, femdom, goddess, headmistress, mastix, mistress, queen.

dominatrix bitch   *n phr* (see etym. note at dominatrix; probably 20th century)   *See* dominatrix   "Experienced dominatrix bitches can fill their stables in no time" (personal interview, "Lucinda," 2/19/87). *Also* amazon (2), bitch goddess, discipliness, dominant bitch, female dominant, femdom, goddess, headmistress, mastix, mistress, queen.

D/S   *n phr* (see etym. notes at dominant and submissive; probably   20th   century)   Dominant*/submissive* "White submissive male (40, novice with some experience) looking for contact with any dominants or submissives (males, females, couples, TV's) in the D/S scene" (*SM Express* no. 24: 12, personal ad).

dual   *n, adj* (probably 20th century)   *See* switchable   "Dual needs slave or master, TV's okay" (personal ad, adult bookstore, Columbus, Ohio, 3/9/87). *Also* middle.

dungeon   *n* (*OED* 14th century, 'secluded chamber, usually in the lowest level of a dwelling, in which prisoners are kept and perhaps tortured'; probably 20th century)   Room containing equipment used by sadomasochists, in which room the sadomasochistic scenario* often occurs   "All fantasies will become reality under my command in my fully equiped [*sic*] dungeon" (*Intimate* 1, no. 1: 29, personal ad). *Also* mardi gras room, playroom, training room.

E   *n, v* Enema*   (*OED*, n, 1681; v probably 20th century)   "Are you M/F? How did you get started? How often do you E? Alone, partner? Give, take? As punishment? Get off? Enjoy most—insertion, retention, expulsion? Favorite E fantasy?" (*Bizarre Lifestyles* no. 84: 31, personal ad).

educate   **1:**   *v*   (*OED* 1841–44, 'teach'; probably 20th century)   Instruct in sadomasochism; show a novice* sadomasochistic procedures and scenarios*   **-ed 2:**   *adj*   (*OED* 1670, 'learned'; probably 20th century)   Being   instructed   as   described   in   sense

1   "Experienced dom looking for willing slaves. Novices okay, can educate" (personal ad, adult bookstore, Columbus, Ohio, 3/11/87).

electric zapper   *n phr* (probably 20th century)   Device similar to the shock box*; the device is used in sadomasochistic relationships and usually has a number of electrodes that may be attached to various parts of the body ("Exquisite Agony," videotape).

enema   *n* (*OED* 1681; *W9* 15th century)   Liquid substance forced up the anus, often followed by insertion of an ass plug*; enemas are usually made of warm water, may surpass two quarts in volume, and are frequently used to induce brown showers* or as a means of discipline* or punishment.* *Also E. See also* forced enema, piss enema, watersports.

enema bandit   *n phr* (see etym. note at enema)   Sadist who typically takes young women as partners and then, as part of the sadomasochistic scenario,* forces an enema into the partner and then immediately has anal sex with him or her (if the sadist is a female, a dildo* is used); this effectively blocks expulsion of the enema and causes a certain amount of pain   As in "This enema bandit shows his partners no mercy, forcing first the you-know-what and then his enormous eleven-inch prick into their assholes" (see "Waterpower," an S & M videotape). *See also* forced enema.

enema discipline   *n phr* (see etym. notes at enema and discipline; probably 20th century)   *See* forced enema. See citation at mild. *Also* forced circulation, forced fluid injection, forced lavage, liquid punishment, liquid torture.

enemy   *n* (*OED* c. 1300)   Penis   "Dominatrix can tame even the biggest and ugliest of enemies—SASE and $5 for info." (personal ad, adult bookstore, Columbus, Ohio, 2/24/87).

English   1:   *n*   (probably   19th   century)   Sadomasochism, especially the spanking, caning, or paddling of
one's   buttocks.   **2:**   *adj*   (probably   20th   century)
Sadomasochistic, as described in sense 1   "English enthusiast, SWM, 34, seeks compatible male" (*Columbus Dispatch*, January 25, 1987, p. 29K, personal ad). *Also* English
arts, English culture, English vice.

English arts   *n phr* (probably 20th century)   *See* English   "Master of the English and Greek arts now accepting
new students" (personal ad, adult bookstore, Columbus,
Ohio, 2/23/87). *Also* English culture, English vice.

English bracelet   *n phr* (probably 20th century)   *See*
studded   cockring   (*CBD*, p. 4, ads for English bracelets).   *Also* English harness C/R, pin prick C/R, spike
bracelet, studded bracelet.

English cock harness   *n phr* (probably 20th century)   Device used in sadomasochistic relationships to
pose and inflict pain on the male masochist's* penis; the harness is usually made of leather and resembles an adjustable
bracelet, but typically has long leather cords attached to it
with a metal ring, which cords can be tied around the waist,
thus elevating the penis for posing, torture, or forced
French.* (*CBD*, p. 3, ads for English cock harnesses). *Also*
cock harness.

English culture   *n phr* (probably 20th century)   *See*
English   "MASCULINE—WM seeks F interested in Eng-
lish/French cultures" (*Columbus Dispatch*, January 25,
1987, p. 29K, personal ad). *Also* English arts, English vice.

English Harness C/R   *n phr* (probably 20th century)   See studded cockring (*CBD*, p. 4, ads for English
harness C/R's. Also English bracelet, pin prick C/R, spike
bracelet, studded bracelet.

English vice   *n phr* (probably 20th century)   *See* English   "TV with interest in English vice would like to meet other TVs with similar interests" (personal ad, adult bookstore, Columbus, Ohio, 3/23/87). *Also* English arts, English culture.

entertain   *v* (*OED* 1490 'receive as a guest'; probably 20th century)   Host sadomasochist relationships in one's home   "Would like to meet bottoms, willing to entertain" (personal ad, adult bookstore, Columbus, Ohio, 1/30/87). *Also* host.

equestrian   *n* (probably 20th century)   *See* equestrian training. See citation at petticoat punishment.

equestrian training   *n phr* (probably 20th century)   Sadomasochistic activities making use of lots of leather items, especially those typically identified with horses (saddle, bridle, riding crop, etc.); frequently includes the sadist riding on the masochist as the latter crawls on hands and legs   "Equestrian training in the woods, naked, helpless and bound between two trees, she lashes his trembling body a beet red. She whips her pony slave into complete submission. The slave becomes her humbled pony slave" (see "Trained Animal" and "Slave Training," videotapes). *Also* equestrian.

equipment   *n* (*OED* 1717, 'furnishings'; probably 20th century)   Toys,* especially those that are large, such as cages,* racks,* bondage tables,* etc.   "Professional dom with years of experience, has well-equipped dungeon with full line of standard toys and equipment" (personal ad, adult bookstore, Columbus, Ohio, 1/30/87).

erotic interrogation   *n phr* (probably 20th century)   Humiliation* and discipline*   "Protracted rituals, erotic interrogation, humiliation, wax, whipping and anal rape make her wanton and wild" (*B & D Pleasures* no. 56: 23, personal ad).

exhibit *v* (*OED* 1529, 'expose or display for view') Display part of a sadomasochistic scenario* in public **-ionism** (*W9* 1893, 'indecent exposure of genitals'; probably 20th century) Sadomasochistic display as described in sense 1 "Submissive wanted for fantasies, incl. mild exhibitionism" (personal ad, adult bookstore, Columbus, Ohio, 1/30/87).

extended ritual *n* (probably 20th century) *See* protracted ritual "Extended rituals are pretty rare. Usually you only see them with people who are really into heavy S & M" (personal interview, "Lucinda," 2/19/87). *Also* prolonged ritual, prolonged scene.

F *n* (probably 20th century) *See* French "Partner needed for F arts, disgression [*sic*] a MUST" (personal ad, restroom wall, OSU main library, 3/11/87). *Also* fr, FR, French art(s), French culture(s). The author of this ad may be punning on *F arts* (*farts*).

face-sitting *n* (probably 20th century) *See* heavy squatting "Hey, cowboy! Face-sitting's my specialty, let me ride yours! No pain, please" (personal ad, adult bookstore, Columbus, Ohio, 2/16/87). *Also* queening.

family affair *n phr* (probably 20th century) Sadomasochistic scenario* involving a married couple and perhaps one or more of their children "Black, 6', 155 lbs., 6½", seeks attractive couples, females, bi-passive males and Pre-op Transsexuals to age 40. Also those interested in Family Affairs. All races" (*Bizarre Lifestyles* 1, no. 1: 41, personal ad).

fantasy *n* (*OED* 1440, 'ingenious or fantastic invention or design') Script of a sadomasochistic scenario,* including whatever both the sadist* and the masochist* agree on; fantasies can range from kidnapping to rape, from castration to murder, from dressing in bizarre costumes to exhibitionism, etc.   "I fulfill all males [*sic*] fetishes and fantasies for my own pleasures" (*Bizarre Lifestyles* 1, no. 1: p. 55, personal ad).

farm slave   *n* (probably 20th century)   Masochist* who becomes bound to the service of his or her sadist,* which service frequently entails a live-in relationship and includes nonsadomasochistic labor   "FARM SLAVE—SALE/RENT: Slave will perform hard labor on farm in exchange for room and board. Owners interested in free labor and who use B/D as a means of training should call. Slave desires to be kept naked, chained, and used by other farm hands at whim" (*Corporal* 10, no. 3: 34, personal ad).

fart-lover   *n* (probably 20th century)   Masochist* who especially enjoys inhaling another's anal gas   "Fart-lover wants yours, possibly B/D also" (personal ad, restroom wall, bar, Columbus, Ohio, 2/23/87).

FD   *n phr* (probably 20th century)   *See* female dominance   "A sensual exploration into the silk and satiny aspects of FD mixed with discipline" (*Women in Command* no. 16: 20, videotape ad).

female dominance   *n phr* (probably 20th century)   Sadomasochistic relationship in which the sadist is a woman and the masochist a man   "English teacher can go both ways, female dominance my specialty" (personal ad, restroom wall, bar, Columbus, Ohio, 3/11/87). *Also* FD.

female dominant   *n phr* (probably 20th century)   Dominatrix*   "Experienced female dominant commands all you slut slaves to contact her at once" (personal ad, adult bookstore, Columbus, Ohio, 1/30/87). *Also* amazon (2), bitch goddess, discipliness, dominant bitch, dominatrix bitch, femdom, goddess, headmistress, mastix, mistress, queen.

femdom   n (probably 20th century)   *See* female dominant   "Fem-dom audio cassette" (*Women in Command* no. 16: 5, audio cassette ad). Also occasionally occurs as hyphenated construction (*fem-dom*). *Also* amazon (2), bitch goddess, discipliness, dominant bitch, dominatrix, dominatrix bitch, goddess, headmistress, mastix, mistress, queen.

feminize   v (*OED* 1652 'make feminine'; probably 20th century)   Force a submissive male to dress in women's lingerie as a means of humiliating* him   "I would like to be feminized and soundly spanked" (*Corporal* 10, no. 3: 38). *See also* forced feminization.

femme   adj (probably 20th century)   Especially pretty lesbian who is interested in sadomasochism   "Looking for femme women for sharing of arts. No TVs, please" (personal ad, adult bookstore, Columbus, Ohio, 4/1/87).

fetish   n (*OED* 1837; 'something irrationally reverenced')   Preoccupation with something, as shoes, feet, etc., and its use in sexual excitation   **-ism**   n (*W9* 1801, *fetishism*)   (See citation at fantasy.)   Fetishes can be developed for anything, though the most common in sadomasochism seem to be for shoes, feet, leather, and rubber.

ff   v, n (probably 20th century) *See* fistfuck,   -ing   "Golden showers, watersports, pt, tt, nt, anal abuse (ff), restraints, butt plugs, toys, etc." (*Mistress* 2, no. 5: 41, personal ad). *Also* fist(ing), handball (ing), handfuck (ing).

financial   donation   n   phr (probably   20th   century)   Payment for sadomasochistic scenario*   "You must be reliable, obedient, prompt, & willing to make financial donations in honor of your mistress" (*Mistress* 2, no. 5: 34, personal ad). *Also* tuition.   *See also* generous, sincere, token. Sadomasochism-for-pay is not as common as ordinary prostitution, but perhaps even more profitable: a well-known, skilled dominatrix can earn hundreds of dollars for a single hour's work.

finger dose *n phr* (Spears 17th century, *finger* 'masturbate the vagina'; probably 20th century) Milder form of fistfucking,* one in which only one or two fingers are used "Slave female, 29, bi, needs your discipline, finger doses (no ff), mild bondage" (personal ad, adult bookstore, Columbus, Ohio, 3/21/87). *Also* finger wave.

fingerfuck 1: *n* (probably 20th century) Milder form of fistfucking* in which only one or two fingers are used rather than the entire hand and forearm. **2:** *v* (probably 20th century) Perform milder form of fistfucking, as described in sense 1 **-ing** *n* (probably 20th century) Process of giving a fingerfuck as explained in sense 1 "Fingerfucking, fistfucking, greek, french, dildoes, enemas, all manner of insertion" (personal ad, adult bookstore, Columbus, Ohio, 3/17/87).

finger rack *n phr* (see etym. note at rack; probably 20th century) Rack* made especially to accommodate and torture the submissive's* fingers "The gallery could now see the thin monofilament line which pulled the finger rack upwards towards two screw eyes into the ceiling beams" (*Women in Command* no. 16: 7, col. 1).

finger wave *n phr* (see etym. note at finger dose; probably 20th century) *See* finger dose "I love sex toys, vibrators [sic], hot lips, long tongues, finger waves & enemas" (*Mistress* 2, no. 5: 7, personal ad).

firelover *n* (probably 20th century) Masochist who derives sexual pleasure from being burned, as with a match "She sniffed the air again. She loved the smell of his burning chest hair and burning flesh. It was like the smell of a good breakfast in the morning, and this was in the afternoon. . . . 'Turn around and offer up your ass . . .' she ordered. The man groaned with gladness and turned slowly. Then he bent forward and said one word. "Firelover" (*Bizarre Lifestyles* no. 84: 22).

firemaster   n (probably 20th century)   Sadist* especially skilled in the use of fire without causing permanent damage to the masochist*   "Experienced firemaster, skilled in all fiery arts, wants YOU firelovers to contact him, male or female, bi okay, no TV's" (personal ad, bar, Columbus, Ohio, 3/13/87).

fist, -ing   v, n (probably 20th century)   *See* fistfuck -ing   "6'2" 190 lbs., blonde/blue, young and hung, submissive muscular male seeks females 18–35 for bondage, mild s/m and possible fisting" (*SM Express* no. 24: 14, personal ad). *Also* ff, handball(ing), handfuck(ing).

fistfuck   v   (Spears 20th century)   Put one's entire fist, a finger at a time, into the vagina or anus; in extreme cases, anal fistfucking can achieve penetration up to the elbow   **-ing**   Behavior as described in sense 1   "I'll fistfuck you into a stupor" (personal ad, restroom wall, bar, Columbus, Ohio, 2/19/87). *Also* ff, fist(ing), handball(ing), handfuck(ing). According to Samois (1979, 5), fistfucking "must be done slowly and carefully, using lots of lubrication. The active partner should also trim [his or] her nails and file them down to nothing to avoid scratching mucous membranes."

fisting club   n phr (probably 20th century)   Group of people, the members of which meet regularly for fistfucking*   As in "Primary fisting club in Midwest, meets once monthly" (see Weinberg, Williams, and Moser 1984, 381).

flagellate   v (*OED* 1623)   Cane, whip, spank, or otherwise beat a masochist   **-ion**   (*OED* 1526)   Behavior described in sense 1   "*Flagellation* is okay, but most people get more turned on with words like *spanking* and *whipping* (personal interview, "Lady in Black," 3/18/87).

According to Samois (1979, 5), flagellation "must be done with great precision. The active partner should never strike the passive partner on the head or neck, the spine or lower back, the throat, or the abdomen."

foot torment   *n phr* (probably 20th century)   Tickling and bondage* of the feet of the submissive*   "S/W/M/ 25, looking for those interested in tight-bondage, s/m, tickling, foot torment, etc." (*B & D Pleasures* no. 56: 28, personal ad).

footworship   *n* (probably 20th century)   Fetish* involving the feet. See citation for equestrian.

force   *v*   (*OED* c. 1300)   In a sadomasochistic scenario,* compel someone to do something against his or her will, which forcing is part of the scenario   **-ed**   (*OED* 1576)   Compelled as described in sense 1   "Dominant female specializing in humiliation, bondage, forced french, fantasy fulfillment, and fetishism" (*Submit* 2, no. 2: 44, personal ad). Most often used in combination with, for example, French,* Greek,* lavage, etc.

forced circulation   *n phr* (probably 20th century)   *See* forced enema   As in "POWER is my game, domination my specialty—forced circulation, humiliation, slavery" (see *Club*, September 1976, p. 88). *Also* enema discipline, forced fluid injection, forced lavage, liquid punishment, liquid torture.

forced enema   *n phr* (see etym. notes at forced, enema; probably 20th century)   Sadomasochistic practice in which an enema* is forcibly given by the sadist to the masochist   "Forced enemas are usually popular with the same people who get into brown and gold showers" (personal interview, "Lucinda," 2/19/87). *Also* enema discipline, forced circulation, forced fluid injection, forced lavage, liquid punishment, liquid torture; *see also* watersports.

forced feminization   *n phr* (see etym. notes at forced, feminize; probably 20th century)   Process of forcing a man to dress up in women's lingerie as a means of humiliation   "Single white submissive male, 30 years old, 140 lbs., 5'11" seeking female domination, bondage, obedience training, forced feminization, total worship of the female body" (*Corporal* 10, no. 3: 38). *See also* feminize; the *forced* in *forced feminization* is redundant.

forced fluid injection   *n phr* (probably 20th century)   *See* forced enema   As in "I'm into forced fluid injection, catheters, Greek, all penetration activities" (see *Club*, September 1976, p. 88). *Also* enema discipline, forced circulation, forced lavage, liquid punishment, liquid torture.

forced French   *n phr* (see etym. notes at forced, French; probably 20th century)   Forced oral sex   "I want to be taught by dominant couples to receive Greek and forced French to completion" (*Intimate* 1, no. 1: 44, personal ad). *Also* forced oral, oral servitude, oral worship.

forced Greek   *n phr* (see etym. notes at forced, Greek; probably 20th century)   Forced anal penetration   "I need a mistress to dominate me with her forced French and forced Greek—NO ROMAN" (personal ad, adult bookstore, Columbus, Ohio, 3/11/87). *Also* ramming.

forced lavage   *n phr* (probably 20th century)   *See* forced enema   "Educated woman into forced lavage seeks docile partner" (personal ad, restroom wall, OSU main library, 2/9/87). *Also* enema discipline, forced circulation, forced fluid injection, forced lavage, liquid punishment, liquid torture.

forced masturbation   *n phr* (see etym. note at forced; *OED* 1766, *masturbation*; probably 20th century)   One person forcing another to masturbate him- or herself, as through the use of whipping, spanking, etc., or the masturbation of another person against that person's will, as when the other person is bound and gagged   "Spanking, humiliation, and forced masturbation are my favorites" (*Bizarre Lifestyles* 1, no. 1: 50, personal ad).

forced oral   *n phr* (probably 20th century)   *See* forced French   "Interests include forced oral, spanking, cock and tit torture" (*SM Express* no. 24: 15, personal ad). *Also* oral servitude, oral worship.

fr   *n* (see etym. note at French; probably 20th century)   *See* French   "Hauntingly beautiful dominant housewife into enemas, body worship, TV, infantilism, Fr, anal, english arts, strict bondage, gags and golden showers, seeks obsequiously docile males requiring total subjugation" (*Bizarre Lifestyles* 1, no. 1: 39, personal ad). *Also* F, FR, French art(s), French culture(s).

FR   *n* (see etym. note at French; probably 20th century)   *See* French   "Into FR, Greek, Roman, all arts, no pain? I want to meat [sic] you! (personal ad, adult bookstore, Columbus, Ohio, 3/28/87). *Also* F, fr, French art(s), French culture(s).

French   *n* (Spears mid–20th century)   Oral sex "Love B/D games (nothing rough), also enjoy french and mild greek" (*Bizarre Lifestyles* 1, no. 1: 41, personal ad). Often occurs uncapitalized. Also F, fr, FR, French art(s), French culture(s).

French art(s)   *n phr* (Rawson 20th century)   *See* French   "I'm SWM, 6'3", 210, 10" hard, and heavily into the French arts; no pain, weirdos, or gays" (personal ad, restroom wall, OSU main library, 2/19/87). Often occurs uncapitalized. Also F, fr, FR, French, French culture(s).

French culture(s)   *n phr* (Rawson 20th century)   *See* French   See citation at English cultures. Often occurs uncapitalized. *Also* F, fr, FR, French, French art(s).

fuck me shoes   *n phr* (probably 20th century)   *See* high heels   "This dom has all the toys you want and need—restraints, fuck me shoes, cuffs, clamps, etc." (personal ad, adult bookstore, Columbus, Ohio, 4/4/87).

fuck tits   *v phr* (probably 20th century)   Masturbation of the penis between the breasts of a female   "Fayetteville white male loves to suck, fuck tits, cunts, wants to try cocks, TS" (*Intimate* 1, no. 1: 43, personal ad). *See also* tit fucking.

G   *n* (see etym. note at Greek; probably 20th century)   *See* Greek   "If you're into alphabet soup as much as I am—F, G, R, etc.—we've got to get together" (personal ad, restroom wall, adult bookstore, Columbus, Ohio, 2/22/87). *Also* backgammon, Gr, GR, Greek, Greek arts, Greek culture.

gag   1:   *n*   (*OED* 1553)   Something put into the mouth of a submissive as a means of discipline* and perhaps humiliation*; the gags may be extremely simple, such as panty gags* or crotch ropes,* or may be more elaborate, such as ball gags* and cock mouth gags* **2:**   *v*   (*OED* 1707)   Stuff something into the mouth as described in sense 1   **-ed**   *adj*   (*OED* 1839)   Disciplined and humiliated as described in sense 1 (*CBD*, p. 6, ad for gags).

games   *n pl* (probably 20th century)   Sadomasochistic activities of all kinds   "Middle-aged housewife, BUILT, bored with life, seeks partner(s) for games—light pain okay, nothing heavy, please" (personal ad, adult bookstore, Columbus, Ohio, 2/22/87).

gangbang   1:   *n*   (Spears, mid–20th century) Combination of sexual intercourse and mild sadomasochism with multiple male partners **2:**   *v* (probably 20th century)   Behave as described in sense 1   "I am seeking males to fulfill gangbang fantasy. I will be bound and blindfolded while servicing up to seven men" (*Intimate* 1, no. 1: 41, personal ad).

gates of hell   *n phr* (probably 20th century)   Device used in sadomasochistic relationships to inflict pain on the masochist's* penis; the device consists of a number of metal rings—each of a smaller diameter than the preceding one—spaced perhaps one-half inch apart and joined by a strip of leather, which rings are slipped over the limp penis and then, when it becomes erect, serve to confine and constrict it (*CLBR*, pp. 4–5, ad for gates of hell).

geisha slave   *n phr* (*W9* 1887, *geisha* 'Japanese girl trained to perform lighthearted entertainment for a man or group of men'; see etym. note at slave; probably 20th century)   Female slave* who receives especially strict punishment* through cuffing, whipping, prodding, poking, etc., at the hands of her usually female master* ("Geisha Slave," title of a videotape).

generous   *adj* (*OED* 1696 'free in giving'; probably 20th century)   Willing to pay for sadomasochistic services   **-ity**   (*OED* 1677, 'readiness or liberality in giving'; probably 20th century)   Payment as described in sense 1   "Dominatrix seeks generous men who desire complete domination and humility" (personal ad, adult bookstore, Columbus, Ohio, 2/23/87).

gentle sex   *n phr* (probably 20th century)   Sadomasochistic activities involving only light pain   "WIMPS DON'T READ THIS! I'm looking for MEN—need PAIN—NO gentle sex, the REAL THING" (personal ad, adult bookstore, Columbus, Ohio, 2/24/87).

gerbil   *v* (*W9* 1849, *gerbil* 'kind of rodent'; probably 20th century)   Insert a gerbil into the anus of a masochist and let it squirm and wiggle until it dies, after which it is removed   **-ing**   *n*   (probably 20th century)   Activity described in sense 1   "Gerbiling started years ago in the gay culture of northern California, but now some S & M people are into it, too. It's really not all that popular" (personal interview, "Lucinda," 2/19/87). *See also* rodent route. The gerbil—minus claws and teeth—is typically inserted into the anus through a tube, one end of which is greased and slid into the anal cavity. Removal of the gerbil is done by pulling on the rodent's tail, which should hang out of the person's anus. That gerbils have somewhat fragile tails is evidenced by the medical literature documenting people being admitted to the emergency room for rodent removal. A similar practice occurred in Vietnam: the Vietcong, as a method of torture, would insert rats into the anuses of their prisoners, teeth and claws intact; the prisoners typically died slow and torturous deaths.

give it up   *v phr* (probably 20th century)   Let oneself be made love to; perform sexual intercourse   "For a lot of people, fucking doesn't even play a role in their excitement; the s/m does it all. But a lot of others got to give it up to be satisfied" (personal interview, "Lucinda," 2/19/87).

gl   *n* (probably 20th century)   Girl   "Want to meet clean people for interesting encounters of the SM kind—bi's and gls only" (personal ad, restroom wall, bar, Columbus, Ohio, 3/30/87).

goddess   *n* (*W9* 14th century, 'female god; woman whose great charm or beauty arouses adoration'; probably 20th century)   *See* dominatrix   "Goddess needs slaves for total submission" (personal ad, restroom wall, Ohio State University main library, 1/19/87). *Also* amazon (2), bitch goddess, discipliness, dominant bitch, dominatrix bitch, female dominant, femdom, headmistress, mastix, mistress, queen.

gold chain   *n phr* (probably 20th century)   Gold-colored metal leash used, for example, in doggie*   "I also like gold chains" (*Women in Command* no. 16: 27, personal ad).

golden   nectar   *n   phr*   (probably   20th   century)

Urine "MILADY'S TOILET SLAVE" Reveals the intimate relationship between her and her golden nectar slave" (*Women in Command* no. 16: 4, audio cassette ad).

golden nuggets *n phr* (probably 20th century) Frozen urine, usually in the form of small pellets, which is thrown at and occasionally sucked on by the masochist in a sado-masochistic scenario* (*Women in Command* no. 16: 8, questionnaire). Also gold nuggets.

golden shower *n phr* (Spears, *golden shower boy* and *golden shower queen* 'male homosexual who enjoys urinating on other homosexuals and/or being urinated on by them,' mid–20th century homosexual use; probably 20th century) Urination on one person by another for the purposes of sexual gratification "ULTRA BIZARRE FEMALE: Age 25, seeks to correspond with submissive men on female domination, foot worship, enema, golden shower and anus worship" (*Bizarre Lifestyles* 1, no. 1: 53, personal ad). *Also* GS, G/S, G.S., pee fun, pissing. *See also* watersports.

gold nuggets *n phr* (probably 20th century) *See* golden nuggets As in "I'll suck on anything my mistress's, including her gold nuggets" (information provided by vice squad, Columbus Police Dept., 3/11/87).

Gr *n, v* (see etym. note at Greek; probably 20th century) *See* Greek "Gr and Fr teacher wanted for intense tutoring" (personal ad, restroom wall, OSU main library, 3/23/87). Also occurs uncapitalized. *Also* backgammon, G, GR, Greek arts, Greek culture.

GR *n, v* (see etym. note at Greek; probably 20th century) *See* Greek "Desire playmate for extended fun and games, esp. GR, B/D, GS" (personal ad, restroom wall, bar, Columbus, Ohio, 4/24/87). *Also* backgammon, G, Gr, Greek arts, Greek culture.

Greek **1:** *n* (Spears mid–20th century) Anal intercourse; a dildo* may be used instead of a penis.

2:   *v*   (probably 20th century)   Have anal intercourse   "33 yr. old, 5'6", versatile TV loves giving prolonged complete French, deep anilingus, passive Greek,
masturbation and your scenes, Straight or Bi-couples, females, TV's, and select hung males" (*Intimate* 1, no. 1: 21,
personal ad). Often uncapitalized. *Also* backgammon, G, Gr,
GR, Greek arts, Greek culture.

Greek arts   *n phr* (see etym. note at Greek; probably 20th
century)   *See* Greek   "Novice TV interested in exploring
all forms of erotica, especially French and Greek arts, with
other TV's" (personal ad, adult bookstore, Columbus, Ohio,
1/29/87). May occur uncapitalized. *Also* backgammon, G, Gr,
GR, Greek culture.

Greek culture   *n phr* (see etym. note at Greek; probably
20th century)   *See* Greek   "I'm uneducated and un-
cultured, but willing to learn. Interested in French, Greek
cultures, light S & M, B/D, GS, etc." (personal ad, restroom
wall, bar, Columbus, Ohio, 3/23/87). *Also* backgammon, G,
Gr, GR, Greek arts.

green   *inter* (probably 20th century)   Safe word* used
to signal the dominant* to proceed in the scenario* (personal
interview, Briar Rose, Women's S/M Support Group, 2/27/
87). *See also* red, yellow.

GS   *n, phr* (see etym. note at golden shower)   *See*
golden shower   "TV into GS and BS, are you there?" (personal ad, restroom wall, bar, Columbus, Ohio, 3/11/87). *Also*
G/S, G.S., pee fun, pissing.

G/S   *n phr* (see etym. note at golden shower)   *See*
golden shower   "Mistress Julie of New York is accepting
slaves who enjoy S&M, B&D, enemas, foot worship, G/S and
related subjects" (*Women in Command*, no. 16: 25, personal
ad). *Also* GS, G.S., pee fun, pissing.

G.S.   *n phr* (see etym. note at golden shower)   *See* golden shower   "My interests are humiliation, public exhibitionism, nipple torture, hot wax, bondage, C & B torture, G.S., all fantasies" (*SM Express* no. 24: 26, personal ad). *Also* GS, G/S, pee fun, pissing.

guidance   *n* (*OED* 1538, 'instruction in conduct or procedure'; probably 20th century)   Direction of a submissive* by his or her master* in various sadomasochistic procedures; a submissive need not necessarily be a novice to receive guidance   "Slave needs guidance by stern master" (personal ad, adult bookstore, Columbus, Ohio, 3/23/87).

H   *n* (see etym. note at humiliation; probably 20th century)   *See* humiliation   "TV into bondage, H, GS, French, Greek, light pain" (personal ad, adult bookstore, Columbus, Ohio, 2/19/87).

hairbrush   **1:**   *n*   (*OED* 1599)   Brush for use on the hair, but adapted by sadomasochists for spanking. **2:**   *v*   (probably 20th century)   Spank with a hairbrush   **-ing**   (probably 20th century)   Spanking with a hairbrush   "Fancy my naughty male bottom flaming red over your knee or across the end of your bed as you spank me to a crisp and whale the tar out of me with a riding crop after the hairbrushing" (*Corporal* 10, no. 3: 34, personal ad).

handball, -ing   *v, n* (probably 20th century)   *See* fistfuck,   -ing   As in "I'm into mild S and M, B and D, some handballing" (see Califia 1980, 111). *Also* ff, fist(ing), handfuck(ing).

handcuff   **1:**   *n*   (*OED* 1775)   Cuff* made specifically to fit on the wrist; handcuffs usually come in pairs and may be separated by a chain or a steel bar of varying length. **2:**   *v*   (*OED* 1720)   Fasten handcuffs to a person's wrists (see citation at ball gag).

handfuck, -ing   υ, n (probably 20th century)   *See* fist-fuck, -ing   "Experienced dom, into handfucking, all wet sex" (personal ad, adult bookstore, Columbus, Ohio, 3/19/87). *Also* ff, fist (ing), handball (ing).

harass   υ (*OED* 1622, 'trouble or vex by repeated attacks'; probably 20th century)   Sadomasochistic procedure in which the sadist* tortures the masochist* through verbal taunts, tickling, and other vexing procedures "Harass me! I crave your punishment of all kinds! Got an urge to taunt, titillate, tickle? Call me!!" (personal ad, adult bookstore, Columbus, Ohio, 3/3/87).

hard labor   n   phr   (probably   20th   century) Sadomasochistic scenario* in which the sadist* forces the masochist* to do various menial tasks, which may include housework, servant's work, etc.   "Slave seeks dominant master who will grind my face into the ground as I do hard labor" (personal ad, adult bookstore, Columbus, Ohio, 4/24/87).

harness C/R   n phr (probably 20th century)   Kind of cock ring,* one with a leather strap or straps or pouch which fits around the waist or testicles; the straps or pouch can be tightened to induce greater pain than that provided by the cockring alone (*The Underground*, ads for harness cockrings).

HD   n phr (probably 20th century)   *See* humiliation, discipline   As in "Professional dominatrix provides all services, HD, SM, GS, anything you want" (information provided by vice squad, Columbus Police Dept., 3/12/87). Also H/D, H.D.

H/D   n phr (probably 20th century)   *See* humiliation, discipline   As in "I'm the Master of all slut slaves who want real H/D" (information provided by vice squad, Columbus Police Dept., 3/12/87). Also HD, H.D.

H.D.   *n phr* (probably 20th century)   *See* humiliation, discipline. See citation at B. Also HD, H/D.

headmistress   *n phr* (see etym. note at mistress; probably 20th century)   *See* dominatrix   "I need a new headmistress, prefer black, for all kinds of bondage and discipline" (personal ad, adult bookstore, Columbus, Ohio, 2/12/87). *Also* amazon (2), bitch goddess, discipliness, dominant bitch, dominatrix bitch, female dominant, femdom, goddess, mastix, mistress, queen.

heavy   *adj* (probably 20th century)   Serious; no-holds-barred   "If you think you can accept the challenge then contact this submissive couple, he in his early fourties [*sic*], she in her middle thirties, have been functioning for over 10 years with some of the heaviest S&M and B&D advocates in the country" (*SM Express* no 24: 13, personal ad). *See also* light.

heavy squatting   *n phr* (probably 20th century)   Face-sitting,* often including urination and/or defecation in addition to French* and anilingus* (*Club*, February 1976, letter column, p. 94). *Also* queening.

helmet   *n* (*OED* 1470–85)   Device that fits over the head of someone in a sadomasochistic relationship; the helmet may be made of metal or leather, and may be made to enhance the appearance of the wearer, to frighten or discipline* the submissive,* etc. (*CBD*, p.7, ad for helmets). *See also* hood.

high heel discipline   *n phr* (see etym. notes at discipline and high heels; probably 20th century)   *See* trampling   "The Goddess teaches him erotic dancing, body worship and high heel discipline" (*Women in Command* no. 16: 14, videotape ad). *Also* high heel training, spike action.

high heels   *n pl* (*OED* 1642, *high-heeled* 'having high heels, as shoes'; probably 20th century)   Women's shoes made with especially high and pointed heels—at least 6 to 9 inches—often used in sadomasochistic scenarios* including shoe fetishes and trampling*; some high heels are made especially for sadomasochistic encounters and may have heels ten inches or more in length (*CBD*, p. 11, ad for high heels). *Also* fuck me shoes.

high heel training   *n phr* (see etym. note at training; probably 20th century)   *See* trampling   "Experienced amazon dominatrix seeking new slaves to undergo high heel training" (personal ad, adult bookstore, Columbus, Ohio, 3/24/87). *Also* high heel discipline, spike action.

hobble skirt   *n phr* (probably 20th century)   Kind of restraint* used in sadomasochistic relationships to restrict the movements of the legs of the submissive*; the restraint is usually made of canvas or leather and worn around the waist like a skirt, but permits only extremely small steps or no steps at all to be taken (see citation for ball gag).

hogties   *n pl* (*W9* 1894, *hogtie* 'tie together the feet of'; probably 20th century)   Bonds used in a sadomasochistic scenario to discipline* or subdue the submissive,* usually by tying the hands and/or feet behind the back; hogties are typically ropes, but may also be chains, lengths of barbed wire, nylon stockings, etc. (see citation for ball gag).

hood   *n* (*OED* c. 700)   Device that fits over the head of someone in a sadomasochistic relationship; the hood is usually made of soft leather or cloth and may be used to enhance the appearance of the wearer, frighten or discipline* the submissive,* etc. (*CBD*, p. 7, ad for hoods). *See also* helmet.

hood bondage   *n phr* (see etym. notes at hood and bondage; probably 20th century)   Specialized form of bondage* involving a tight hood* that applies pressure to all parts of the head and sometimes the neck simultaneously (*CBD*, p. 8, ad for hoods; see also *B & D Pleasures* no. 56: 31, picture).

horizontal bra   *n phr* (*OED* 1936, *bra*; probably 20th century)   Device used in sadomasochistic relationships to inflict pain on the female masochist's* breasts; the horizontal bra, made similar to a standard brassiere but of metal and leather, is so constructed as to be able to stretch the breasts away from each other (*B & D Pleasures* no. 56: 29, ad for horizontal bra).

horse   *n* (*OED* 1703, 'frame or structure on which something is mounted or supported'; *OED* 1718, 'sawhorse'; probably 20th century)   Device used in sadomasochism to support the sadist in such a position that his or her buttocks are facing up; typically the sadist straddles the device and has his or her head pointing toward the floor   "Complete line of B&D equipment—horizontal and vertical bras, breast presses, horses of all sizes, whips, chains, gags, buttplugs, etc." (ad, adult bookstore, Columbus, Ohio, 2/13/87). *See also* on the moon.

host   *v* (*OED* 1485, 'receive into one's house and entertain'; probably 20th century)   *See* entertain   "Can travel or host" (personal ad, restroom wall, bar, Columbus, Ohio, 3/11/87).

hot turds   *n phr* (probably 20th century)   *See* brown shower   "Hot turds, golden showers, soapy enemas and my hot dildo cock is ready for your ass!" (*Corporal* 10, no. 3: 35 personal ad). *Also* Boston tea party, BS, B/S, scat.

hot wax   *n phr* (probably 20th century)   *See* candle wax torture. See citation at G.S. *Also* wax, wax torture.

housemaid   *n* (*OED* 1694, 'female domestic servant'; probably 20th century)   *See* maid   "Strict Mistress England requires all you low queen toilet slaves to write. On your low status as housemaids, domestics under strict women [*sic*]. Scrubbing floor, aproned caned [*sic*] for any slack housework" (*B & D Pleasures* no 56: 26, personal ad).

humble   *v* (*OED* 1591, 'render meek in spirit'; probably 20th century)   *See* humiliate   "Toilet slave needs to be humbled by dominant master" (personal ad, adult bookstore, Columbus, Ohio, 1/29/87).

humiliate   *v*   (*OED* 1533–34)   Deliberately lower the status of the submissive* in a sadomasochistic relationship, usually through emotional and/or psychological means; humiliation is the psychological counterpart to physical pain. *Also* humble **-ion**   *n*   (*OED* 1386)   Lowering of one's status as described in sense 1   "We will humiliate, humble and harass" (*Intimate* 1, no. 1: 28, personal ad). Humiliation is frequently used in personal ads as a feature to attract potential partners; an example of humiliation is "Are you afraid, scumbag? . . . Well, you should be, faggot! I'm your goddess! Your punishment mistress! I own you, sissy boy! You are mine! You are a degenerate worm, and I am condescending to give you my attention, which you certainly do not deserve!" (*Bizarre Lifestyles* no. 84: 12). *Also* H. Frequently used in combination with discipline*; *see also* HD, H/D, H.D.

hustle   *v* (Spears early 20th century underworld usage, 'work as a prostitute'; probably 20th century)   Solicit sadomasochism for pay   **-ing**   *n*   (probably 20th century)   Activity of soliciting sadomasochism for pay   "Sure lots of us hustle. You got to make a living, you know?" (personal interview, "Lucinda," 2/19/87).

ice cube   *n phr* (probably 20th century)   Small cube of ice placed on the body of (usually blindfolded or hooded) masochists* during sadomasochistic scenarios*; the effect of ice cubes on the body is indistinguishable from that of hot wax, at least momentarily   As in "We provide all modern tortures, from ice cubes to hot wax to all standard paraphernalia" (see Califia, 1980, 130). *See also* candle wax torture.

indoor sports *n phr* (probably 20th century) Sadomasochistic activities of any kind "Indoor sports enthusiast desires meetings with rubber, leather aficionados" (personal ad, adult bookstore, Columbus, Ohio, 3/22/87).

infantilism *n* (*W9* 1895, 'retention of childish qualities in adult life') Kind of humiliation,* one in which the submissive* is treated like a baby, perhaps to the extent of being forced to wear diapers on which the dominant has already urinated and/or defecated "As nurse, train babies (adults) to beg for titty bottles. Change of diaper and wet rubber pants. Bedwetter well thrashed and catherized [*sic*]. Full public humiliations sucking pacifier. Bibs on and pinafores" (*B & D Pleasures* no. 56: 26, personal ad).

infibulate *v* (*OED* 1623, 'fasten with a ring or clasp') Fasten a ring or clasp to the sexual organs, including the breasts, the penis and testicles, and the labia **-ion** *n* (*OED* 1650, 'fastening with a ring or clasp, especially the sexual organs) Fastening or clasping as described in sense 1 As in "Educated man seeks curious lady for infibulation" (see *Club*, August 1976, p. 98, letter column).

Irish *n* (probably 20th century) Especially forceful sadomasochistic scenario* or partner; *Irish* typically denotes violence and blood "Anyone out there into strong Irish? I command you to call me! Weaklings and the squeamish need NOT apply" (personal ad, adult bookstore, Columbus, Ohio, 4/3/87). *See also* beat the brains out.

ivory rinse *n phr* (probably 20th century) Ejaculation of a male sadomasochist onto his partner(s) "Scumbag needed to revel in repeated ivory rinses, forced masturbation, must swallow all" (personal ad, adult bookstore, Columbus, Ohio, 2/22/87).

jism   *n*   (probably   20th   century   or   before)   Semen   "Seeks studs to satisfy her nymphom-
aniac desires. Black cock, hot pussies, pee fun, Greek, eating
hot jism, and doggie peter are a few of the things that will
satisfy her insatiable lusts" (*Intimate* 1, no. 1: 25, personal
ad).

JO   *v* (probably 20th century)   Jack-off session; period
of time during which all the participants in a given scenario*
masturbate   themselves   and/or   one   another
JOer   *n*   (probably 20th century)   Jack-offer; one
who especially enjoys jack-off sessions as described in sense
1   "JOers okay; my wife and I have regular JOs" (personal
ad, adult bookstore, Columbus, Ohio, 1/21/87).

kennel discipline   *n phr* (probably 20th century)   *See*
doggie   "My fantasy is to be treated like a dog; anyone out
there into kennel discipline?" (personal ad, adult bookstore,
Columbus, Ohio, 1/30/87). *Also* kennel training.

kennel training   *n phr* (probably 20th century)   *See*
doggie   "New master in town now accepting slaves for advanced kennel training" (personal ad, adult bookstore, Columbus, Ohio, 1/19/87). *Also* kennel discipline.

key-word   *n*   (probably   20th   century)   *See* safe
word   "The thing about key-words is, you got to get the
dominant to recognize and respect them—and a lot of them
don't" (personal interview, "Lucinda," 2/19/87).

kidnap   *v* (*OED* 1682, 'abduct a person against his or her
will'; probably 20th century)   In a sadomasochistic scenario,* role-played fantasy in which the dominant* abducts
the submissive* against his or her will   **-ing**   *n* (*OED*
1682; probably 20th century)   Process of abduction, as
explained in sense 1   "Don't call me unless you want every
fantasy and fetish fulfilled—shoes, heels, kidnapping, rape,

etc." (personal ad, adult bookstore, Columbus, Ohio, 2/22/87).

kink   *n* (*OED* 19th century, 'mental twist'; probably 20th century)   Unusual or bizarre fetish, or person having such a fetish   **-y**   *adj* (*OED* 1860, 'queer, eccentric'; probably 20th century)   "Satisfy all needs, cater to all kinks—nothing too weird or bizarre" (personal ad, restroom wall, OSU main library, 3/19/87).

kinky sex   *n phr* (see etym. note at kinky; probably 20th century)   Kinky* sadomasochistic activities "Professional dom can satisfy your urge to be controlled; kinky sex is my specialty!" (personal ad, adult bookstore, Columbus, Ohio, 3/11/87).

kitty   *n* (probably 20th century)   Small cat-o-nine-tails*   (*CBD*, p. 7, ad for kitties). *Also* mini cat.

labia ring   *n phr* (probably 20th century)   Piercing ring that fits through the labia of the submissive*; labia rings can be used both to induce pain and to play out the fantasy of chastity belts (*CBD*, p. 9, ad for labia rings).

lacing bar   *n phr* (probably 20th century)   Steel or wooden rod, of varying length, typically used to lash the arms or legs of a submissive* to; the lacing bar is usually placed behind the knees or the back and can render the bound limbs quite motionless   "Marianne took me by the hand and led me to the the largest of six storage sheds. Upon entering it had become quite clear that she had already made several preparations. A corset lacing bar hung from a chain connected to a pulley. I had seen that lacing bar before. I [*sic*] was an antique that mother use [*sic*] to keep hanging over the foot of her bed. I didn't understand what my mother did for a living at the time. Looking back, I'm sure many men have paid handsomely to hang from that bar" (*SM Express* no. 24: 9, cols. 2–4).

leash   *n* (*OED* c. 1300)   Length of leather or chain extending from a collar* on the neck of a submissive* to some permanent fixture or the hand of the dominant*; leashes are used in doggie* and other discipline scenarios* (*CLBR*, p. 2, ad for leashes).

leather   *n* (Spears 20th century, 'pertaining to any sadistic male')   Sadomasochism or sadomasochistic activities   "I am queen of all leather, bar none" (personal ad, restroom wall, bar, Columbus, Ohio, 3/30/87). Often used in combination, as in leather bar,* leather man,* leather sex,* etc.; *Leather Underground* is the name of a newspaper catering to people interested in sadomasochism of all kinds. *Also* leather/rubber, leather scene, leather sex.

leather bar   *n phr* (etym. note at leather; probably 20th century)   Bar known for the sadomasochistic tendencies of its patrons   "Meet me at the leather bar [address given]" (personal ad, restroom wall, OSU main library, 3/23/87).

leather bath   *n phr* (see etym. note at leather; probably 20th century)   *See* leather club   "Novice needs leather bath" (personal ad, restroom wall, bar, Columbus, Ohio, 4/14/87).

leather club   *n phr* (see etym. note at leather; probably 20th century)   Gathering place for people interested in sadomasochism, perhaps the best known of which is New York City's Loft   "Columbus ain't got no leather clubs! I'm from NY, where there's Loft [*sic*], now *that's* a leather club" (editorial, restroom wall, bar, Columbus, Ohio, 3/23/87). *Also* leather bath.

leather dyke   *n phr* (see etym. note at leather; probably 20th century)   Lesbian interested in sadomasochism who has a fetish* for leather*   "Single female, 23, well stacked, seeks partner for exploration of french and greek cultures. Leather dykes preferred" (personal ad, adult bookstore, Columbus, Ohio, 3/30/87).

leather man   *n phr* (see etym. note at leather; probably 20th century)   **1:** Male sadomasochist   "King leather man now available for all willing, durable sluts brave enough to try me!" (personal ad, adult bookstore, Columbus, Ohio, 3/3/87).   **2:**   *See* leather queen   "Leather man looking for his queen to have meaningful relationship with" (personal ad, restroom wall, bar, Columbus, Ohio, 1/22/87).

leather queen   *n phr* (Spears 20th century homosexual usage, 'aggressive and possibly sadistic male homosexual who wears leather clothing'; probably 20th century)   Male homosexual interested in sadomasochism   "Male, 5'10", 11" hard, 190 lbs., looking for possible SM partners for forced french and greek—no leather queens, please" (personal ad, adult bookstore, Columbus, Ohio, 3/30/87). *Also* leather man (2).

leather/rubber   *n phr* (see etym. note at leather; probably 20th century)   *See* leather   "Novice wants into the leather/rubber scene, but needs experienced teacher" (personal ad, adult bookstore, Columbus, Ohio, 2/22/87). *Also* leather scene, leather sex, L/R.

leather scene   *n phr* (see etym. note at leather; probably 20th century)   *See* leather   "Want to be part of the leather scene but don't know who to turn to? Call Marianne [phone number]" (personal ad, adult bookstore, Columbus, Ohio, 3/15/87). *Also* leather/rubber, leather sex, L/R.

leather sex   *n phr* (see etym. note at leather; probably 20th century)   *See* leather   "Leather sex specialist, call Rob" (personal ad, restroom wall, bar, Columbus, Ohio, 3/23/87). *Also* leather/rubber, leather scene, L/R.

leather strap   *n phr* (*W9, leather* [before 12th century] + *strap* [1573])   Piece of leather, perhaps twisted and with a handle, used for whippings and floggings in sadomasochistic scenarios* (*CBD*, p. 5, ad for leather straps).

left hip pocket   *n phr* (probably 20th century)   *See* master   "My left hip pocket is gone, and I need a new one! NOW!" (personal ad, adult bookstore, Columbus, Ohio, 4/11/ 87). Rare. When a handkerchief is worn in the left hip pocket in an S and M bar, it is a visual signal that the wearer is a master looking for a slave.* *Also* corporalist, dom, dominant, M (3), S (2), sadist, sender, sir, taskmaster, top. *See also* right hip pocket.

legbinder   *n* (probably 20th century)   Device used in sadomasochistic relationships to bind the legs of the masochist*; the legbinder may be made of leather, rope, chain, or barbed wire, and usually binds the legs to one another, perhaps with the aid of a lacing stick* (*CBD*, p. 7, ad for legbinders). *See also* armbinder.

leg spreaders   *n phr* (probably 20th century)   Kind of manacle for the legs, one in which, usually, two steel bands are fastened to the ankles and separated by a steel bar of varying length; the effect is to prevent the legs from coming together   "Next she strapped as [*sic*] what I now know are leg spreaders on my ankles" (*SM Express* no. 24: 9).

light   *adj* (*OED* c. 950, 'easy to bear or endure'; probably 20th   century)   Not   heavy*;   containing   minimal pain   "Male, married with willing partner, seeking third party or second couple for greek, roman, light B/D" (personal ad, adult bookstore, Columbus, Ohio, 3/23/87). *See also* heavy, mild.

light blue handkerchief   *n phr* (probably 20th century)   Person with a preference for oral (as opposed, for example, to anal) sex   "Need light blue handkerchief for regular get-togethers" (personal ad, restroom wall, OSU main library, 4/22/87).   The light blue handkerchief, when worn so that it is visible to the public in an S and M bar, is a visual signal that the wearer is looking for a partner to share oral activities.

limits *n pl* (*OED* c. 1375, *limit* 'boundary, frontier'; probably 20th century) Outermost boundary of pain willing to be tolerated by a masochist* "Limits observed" (*B & D Pleasures* no. 56: 26, personal ad).

liquid punishment *n phr* (see etym. note at punishment; probably 20th century) *See* forced enema "DIAPERS & ENEMAS, a series of cuddly adult babies get disciplined with sound spankings and then their round mounds are given liquid punishment, including one male whose black ass really writhes in rhythm" (*B & D Pleasures* no. 56: 27, videotape ad). *Also* enema discipline, forced circulation, forced fluid injection, forced lavage, liquid torture.

liquid torture *n phr* (see etym. note at torture; probably 20th century) *See* forced enema "White male into all water sports, liquid tortures, etc." (personal ad, restroom wall, Larry's Bar, Columbus, Ohio, 3/19/87). *Also* enema discipline, forced circulation, forced fluid injection, forced lavage, liquid punishment.

love arts *n phr* (probably 20th century) *See* arts "Can service couples. Am a master of love arts" (*Intimate* 1, no. 1: 27 personal ad).

L/R *n phr* (see etym. note at leather/rubber; probably 20th century) *See* leather/rubber "Female, novice to world of L/R, needs experienced teacher, male or bi, for intensive tutoring sessions" (personal ad, adult bookstore, Columbus, Ohio, 4/14/87). *Also* leather, leather scene, leather sex.

M *n* (probably 20th century) **1:** *See* masochism "Conservative sadist needs a little more M in his life" (adult bookstore, Columbus, Ohio, 4/2/87) *Also* pagan worship. **2:** *See* masochist "Female M needs dominated by YOU" (adult bookstore, Columbus, Ohio, 2/24/87). *Also* bottom, passive, right hip pocket, S (3), slave, sub, submissive. **3:**   *See* master   "If you're looking for real pain, call me and let me be your M" (adult bookstore, Columbus, Ohio, 1/30/87).   *Also* corporalist, dom, dominant, left hip pocket, S (2), sadist, sender, sir, taskmaster, top. (The second definition is common everywhere except the West Coast; the third definition prevails only on the West Coast. See note 5 in the prefatory matter to this glossary.)

mackintosh fun   *n phr* (probably 20th century) Fetish* involving rubber, especially rubber raincoats   As in "Gentleman desirous of meeting lady for adult mackintosh fun" (information provided by *Club*, April 1975, Karl Steiner column).

maid   *n*   (*OED* 1390, 'female servant or attendant'; probably 20th century)   Kind of humiliation*, one in which usually a man is made to dress up like a maid and do menial tasks   "One of my favorite [fantasies] is to be an exposed maid or servant. I love to wear only garterbelts, nylons, high heels and cook, clean, serve drinks, and masturbate while being able to be watched" (*Intimate* 1, no. 1: 53, personal ad). *Also* housemaid; *see also* maid service, servant.

maid servant   *n phr* (see etym. note at maid; probably 20th century)   What a maid* does in the course of humiliation,* including household tasks and the fulfillment of whatever his or her master* wishes   "New slave needed for strict maid service" (personal ad, restroom wall, bar, Columbus, Ohio, 2/12/87).

M and M   *n phr* (probably 20th century)   Mutual masturbation; the simultaneous masturbation of two or more people by each other   "Female, built, looking for adventurous partner for M and M forced french, maybe greek" (personal ad, adult bookstore, Columbus, Ohio, 3/23/87).

mardi gras room   *n phr* (*W9* 1699, *Mardi Gras* 'New Orleans celebration'; probably 20th century)   *See* dungeon   "Mistress Destiny laughed outwardly at the antics of her two slaves. She sort of surmised that the slut had found out who had found out [*sic*] who had forgotten to tell her that 'last one into the mardi gras room' was in line for a session" (*Women in Command*, no. 16, p. 7). *Also* dungeon, playroom, training room.

mask   *n* (*OED* 1534)   Device worn on the face of a participant in a sadomasochistic relationship, which device covers the area of the face around the eyes and nose while still allowing the wearer to see through holes cut for the eyes; masks are usually tied behind the wearer's head, are typically made of soft leather, and may be adorned with small chains, studs, etc. (*CLBR*, p. 6, ad for masks).

masochism   *n* (*OED* 1893)   Delight in being dominated by another, called a sadist,* often to the point of receiving pain and torture. *Also* M (1), pagan worship.   **-ist** *n*   (probably 20th century)   Person taking delight of the kind described in sense 1   "Masochism is a tough thing to define in absolute terms, you know? I mean, when does pleasure stop and pain start for the average person?" (personal interview, "Lucinda," 2/19/87). *Also* bottom, M (2), passive, right hip pocket, S (3), slave, sub, submissive.

master   *n* (*OED* 15th century, 'owner of a living creature'; *OED* c. 1400, 'possessor, owner')   Male sadist* in a sadomasochistic relationship; one who dominates a submissive* or slave*   "I command you to call me! Experienced master now considering applications for slut slaves" (personal ad, adult bookstore, Columbus, Ohio, 3/26/87). *Also* corporalist, dom, dominant, left hip pocket, M (3), S (2), sadist, sender, sir, taskmaster, top.

mastix   *n* (probably 20th century)   Female sadist* As in "Mastix for hire, plenty of experience, satisfy all fantasies" (information provided by vice squad, Columbus Police Dept., 3/11/87). Rare. *Also* amazon (2), bitch goddess, discipliness, dominant bitch, dominatrix, dominatrix bitch, female dominant, femdom, goddess, headmistress, mistress, queen.

masturbation punishment   *n phr* (see etym. note at punishment; probably 20th century)   Punishment* in which the dominant* repeatedly masturbates the submissive,* or has the submissive masturbate him- or herself, perhaps without allowing orgasm   "I decided upon masturbation punishment. For thirty minutes I made her play with herself (in wrist cuffs) for me, which she found quite humiliating" (*Corporal* 10, no. 3: 14).

mate-training   *n phr* (probably 20th century) Domination of one's mate or partner by another; mate-training always refers to three-or-more-person scenarios*   "Looking for couple to share mate-training" (personal ad, adult bookstore, Columbus, Ohio, 4/2/87).

mature   *adj* (*OED* 1600, 'having the powers of the body fully developed')   Of a woman, having especially large breasts and buttocks; of a man, having an especially large penis and testicles   "Mature, strikingly beautiful and refined Women's Libber, who believes unreservedly that the male should be restricted to his rightful place, desires contact with educated gentlemen genuinely interested in mysticism and pagan worship. No time wasters or weaklings" (*Club*, March 1977, p. 22, Karl Steiner glossary of implications of words in S & M advertisements). *Mature* may also be coming to mean 'middle-aged or older': one professional dominatrix in Akron, Ohio, uses the term to advise potential customers that she is 60+ years old.

meat tenderizer   *n phr* (probably 20th century)   Device intended to help adorn and inflict pain on the penis of the masochist* in a sadomasochistic relationship; meat tenderizers typically consist of a triangular piece of leather—with a hole in the middle through which the penis protrudes—connected to chains in the fashion of a standard athletic supporter (*CLBR*, p. 3, ad for meat tenderizers).

mercy   n (*OED* 1225)   Quality of being kind or compassionate; having pity   "I want to serve you—ram your dick or dildo up my ass, I can take up to 12"—show me no mercy" (personal ad, OSU main library, 2/17/87). *Mercy* is frequently used as a safe word* to indicate that the submissive* believes the sadomasochistic scenario* is getting out of hand.

middle   n (probably 20th century)   *See* dual   "I'm primarily a slave, but can be middle" (personal ad, adult bookstore, Columbus, Ohio, 3/12/87). *Also* switchable.

mild   adj (*OED* c. 725)   Not harsh or severe   "Anal penetration, mild enema discipline desirable, but not required" (*Corporal* 10, no. 3: 36 personal ad). *Mild* is frequently used in personal ads to indicate that the advertiser is only marginally interested in the activity described, or is experimenting with the activity described for the first time. *See also* light.

milk   n (Spears 17th century)   Semen   "Cum freak wants to drink your milk" (personal ad, adult bookstore, Columbus, Ohio, 3/31/87).

milking   n (see etym. note at milk; probably after 17th century)   Repeated masturbation of a male masochist*   "I'm into bondage and discipline, gags, all fetishes, milking, french, greek, roman, even pets" (personal ad, adult bookstore, Columbus, Ohio, 3/23/87).

mini cat   n (see etym. note at cat-o-nine-tails; probably 20th century)   *See* kitty   (*B & D Pleasures*, no. 56, p. 29, ad for mini cats).

mistress   n (*OED* 1380, 'woman who has the power or control to dispose of something'; *OED* 1374, 'instructress'; probably 20th century)   *See* dominatrix   "Mistress looking for others with interests in spanking, french worship and leather training, also B&D" (*Bizarre Lifestyles* 1, no. 1:

47 personal ad). Frequently used in combination with the mistress's first name or pseudonym, as in "Mistress Stephane." *Also* amazon (2), bitch goddess, discipliness, dominant bitch, dominatrix bitch, female dominant, femdom, goddess, headmistress, mastix, queen.

mitten   *n* (*OED* 1386)   Device used in sadomasochistic relationships, usually for spanking, which device is worn on the hand and encases the four fingers together and the thumb separately; mittens come in a wide variety of styles—they may, for example, be studded with metal protrusions or faced with a soft fur (*CBD*, p. 8, ad for mittens).

mole   *n* (Spears 19th century, 'penis'; probably 20th century; perhaps from *Mohel* 'ritual circumcision performed on Jewish infants')   **1:**   Female dominant who, as part of her sadomasochistic scenarios,* regularly slits or pierces the penis of her male masochists.* **2:**   Penis slit or pierced as described in sense 1. **3:**   Man with a penis slit or pierced as described in sense 1   As in "Experienced dom seeks potential moles" (information provided by vice squad, Columbus Police Dept., 3/11/87).

mummy   *n* (*OED* 1615, 'corpse preserved through mummification'; probably 20th century)   Submissive* confined by being completely wrapped up, as in plastic wrap   **-ification**   *n*   (*OED* 1800, 'process of preserving corpse by making it into a mummy'; probably 20th century)   Confinement of a submissive as explained in sense 1   "Into most fetishes, all fantasies, incl. domination, mummification, doggie, etc." (personal ad, adult bookstore, Columbus, Ohio, 4/13/87).

nameless crime   *n phr* (probably 20th century) Unspecified sadomasochistic activities   "SWM would like to meet SWF or MWF for mutual enjoyment of nameless crimes, including greek and french" (personal ad, adult bookstore, Columbus, Ohio, 3/23/87).

naughty boy *n phr* (Spears 19th century, *naughty* 'copulation'; Spears mid–16th century, *naughty* 'obscene, smutty'; probably 20th century)   *See* bad boy "Mistress Stephane desires contacts with Naughty boys, spankings, foot worship" (*Women in Command* no. 16: 29, personal ad).

niece   *n* (probably 20th century)   Dominant* role* played by a female or crossdressing male in a sadomasochistic scenario*   "Stimulating correspondence sought with long-lost strict aunt, or spoiled, sassy niece" (*Corporal* 10, no. 3: 36, personal ad).

nipple bondage   *n phr* (probably 20th century)   *See* breast torture   "Nipple bondage can include almost any kind of torture to the breasts, including, of course, piercing the nipples and inserting a ring that can then have a heavy chain attached to it" (personal interview, Briar Rose, S/M Women's Support Group, Columbus, Ohio, 2/27/87). *Also* breast torture, nipple breast bondage, nipple discipline, nipple restraint, nipple torture, nt, tit bondage, tit discipline, tit torture, titty bondage, titty discipline, titty torture, tt.

nipple breast bondage   *n phr* (probably 20th century)   *See* breast torture   "Submissive wife available to male dominants [*sic*] B & D games, nipple breast bondage" (*SM Express* no. 24: 14, personal ad). *Also* breast torture, nipple bondage, nipple discipline, nipple restraint, nipple torture, nt, tit bondage, tit discipline, tit torture, titty bondage, titty discipline, titty torture, tt.

nipple clamp   *n phr* (probably 20th century)   Device used in sadomasochistic scenarios* to inflict pain on the nipples of the masochist*; the device is a small clamp that fits onto the nipple and which may be attached to a variety of ropes, chains, wall fixtures, etc. ("Exquisite Agony," videotape).

nipple cords   *n phr* (probably 20th century)   Pieces of thin rope or heavy string attached to the submissive's* nipples, usually by piercing rings; the other end of the cords may be attached to screw eyes, pulleys, etc., but in any case are positioned so as to allow great tension to be put on the nipples   "When the fingers and nipple cords had been properly positioned high overhead, the two lines were joined" (*Women in Command* no. 16: 7, col. 1).

nipple cuff   *n phr* (see etym. note at cuff; probably 20th century)   *See* nipple ring   "NIPPLE CUFFS: Would you like to give your lover a pleasant and sensuous surprise? If so, why not purchase a pair of Nipple Cuffs for your lady?" (*B & D Pleasures* no. 56: 25, ad for nipple cuffs).

nipple discipline   *n phr, v* (probably 20th century) *See* breast torture   "Oh, I don't get into stuff like nipple discipline and penis torture; I'm strictly legit; I only talk dirty over the telephone" (personal interview, "Lucinda," 2/19/87). *Also* breast torture, nipple bondage, nipple breast bondage, nipple restraint, nipple torture, nt, tit bondage, tit discipline, tit torture, titty bondage, titty discipline, titty torture, tt.

nipple restraint   *n phr* (probably 20th century)   *See* breast torture   "Nipple restraint my specialty. I have the biggest collection of clamps, presses, and chains you've ever seen!" (personal ad, restroom wall, bar, Columbus, Ohio, 4/2/87). *Also* breast torture, nipple bondage, nipple breast bondage, nipple discipline, nipple torture, nt, tit bondage, tit discipline, tit torture, titty bondage, titty discipline, titty torture, tt.

nipple ring   *n phr* (probably 20th century)   Adjustable, usually nonpiercing ring placed around the nipple and tightened; helps create and sustain nipple erections and also causes pain   "NIPPLE RINGS: The World's [*sic*] most sensuous jewelry keeps nipples erect" (*Corporal* 10, no. 3, p. 25, ad for nipple rings). *Also* nipple cuff.

nipple torture   *n phr, v* (probably 20th century)   *See* breast torture   "Enjoy B & D, nipple torture, whippings and many forms of pain and humiliation" (*B & D Pleasures* no. 56: 20, personal ad). *Also* breast torture, nipple bondage, nipple breast bondage, nipple discipline, nipple restraint, nt, tit bondage, tit discipline, tit torture, titty bondage, titty discipline, titty torture, tt.

nt   *n phr* (probably 20th century)   *See* breast torture   "Married white couple, late 30's, she-dominant, he-submissive, enjoy off beat and kinky sex play. Golden showers, watersports, pt, tt, nt, anal abuse (ff), restraints, butt plugs, toys, etc." (*Mistress* 2, no. 5: 41, personal ad). *nt* is an abbreviation of nipple torture. *Also* breast torture, nipple bondage, nipple breast bondage, nipple discipline, nipple restraint, nipple torture, tit bondage, tit discipline, tit torture, titty bondage, titty discipline, titty torture, tt.

nylon cat   *n phr* (see etym. note at cat; probably 20th century)   Cat-o-nine-tails made specifically out of nylon (*B & D Pleasures* no. 56: 29, ad for nylon cats).

obedience   *n* (*OED* 1225)   Strict willingness by a masochist* to do what a sadist* commands or requires, within the confines of a scenario*   **-ient**   *adj*   (*OED* 1225)   Having the quality of obeyance as specified in sense 1   "Dominant female now accepting applications for slavery from all slut males who believe they qualify—obedience a must" (personal ad, adult bookstore, Columbus, Ohio, 4/12/87).

obedience training   *n phr* (see etym. notes at obedience and train; probably 20th century)   Sadomasochistic activities including bondage, whipping, and other disciplinary measures. See citation at forced feminization. *Also* sextraining, training.

on the moon   *prep phr* (probably 20th century) Strapped, chained, or tied to a horse* "Another slave spent the day on the moon as it was called. She was strapped over a device that stood her ass in the air and was treated to a long dildo into her ass with everybody watching" (*Women in Command* no. 16: 6, col. 1). Construction is strange, since *moon* does not apparently exist as a synonym for *horse* (though it has existed as a synonym for *buttocks* in *shoot the moon* and *to moon* since the mid—20th century); probably *on the moon* is as much a description of the person's physical and psychological threshold of pain as a description of the person's position on the horse.

open swinging   *n phr* (Spears mid—20th century, *swing* 'be involved in sexual fads or group sex'; probably 20th century)   Sadomasochistic activities among an unspecified number of participants, the number and identity of which may change from scenario* to scenario   "Bored housewife needs a little excitement! Would like to get into open swinging, if possible. No heavy pain, but willing to try most anything else twice!" (personal ad, adult bookstore, Columbus, Ohio, 2/27/87).

oral adoration   *n phr* (probably 20th century)   Oral sex allowed to be given by a submissive* to his or her dominant* as a reward for being especially obedient   "Oral adoration as reward" (*Women in Command* no. 16: 8, questionnaire). *See also* rewards of worship, of which oral adoration is one.

oral servitude   *n phr* (probably 20th century)   *See* forced French   "I like bondage, teasing, oral servitude, discipline, leather, rubber and whatever you like" (*B & D Pleasures* no. 56: 26, personal ad). *Also* forced oral, oral worship.

oral worship   *n phr* (probably 20th century)   Exceedingly strong oral servitude*   "Am into B & D, nipple bondage, oral worship, mild greek, some pets" (personal ad, restroom wall, bar, Columbus, Ohio, 3/23/87). *Also* forced French, forced oral.

orange handkerchief   *n phr* (probably 20th century)   Sadomasochistic relationship in which anything is

allowed, or a person in such a relationship   "Orange handkerchiefs eat quiche!" (graffito, restroom wall, OSU main library, 2/24/87). In an S and M bar, a person wearing an
orange handkerchief is advertising for an "anything goes"
partner.

own   *v*   (*OED* c. 888)   Claim as a possession, as between a dominant* and his or her slave*   -ed   *adj* (*OED*
1583)   Claimed as a possession, especially as specified in
sense 1   "I will own you, body and soul, will make you
whimper with pain and delight, will force you to cater to my
every need, then trample you into the dirt where you belong"
(personal ad, adult bookstore, Columbus, Ohio, 3/12/87).

ownership   *n* (*OED* 1583 'fact or state of being an owner';
probably 20th century)   Sadomasochistic relationship, as
between a dominant* and submissive,* involving extreme
bondage and discipline, and perhaps ultimately a permanent
relationship between the two partners   "Very bi submissive slut wishes to meet dominant mistress for total training
as slave interested in humiliation, toilet training, B&D and
ownership" (*B & D Pleasures* no. 56: 21, personal ad).

paddle   **1:**   *n*   (*OED* 1828)   Device used in sadomasochistic relationships, usually by the sadist* in an attempt to inflict pain on the buttocks of the masochist*
through spanking; paddles come in a variety of styles, but
are usually made of wood and/or stiff leather and often have
air holes cut in them to cut down on air resistance.
2:   *v*   (*OED* 1856)   Use a device as described in sense
1   (*CBD*, p. 7, ad for paddles).

pagan worship   *n phr* (probably 20th century)   *See*
masochism   See citation for mature. *Also* M (1).

page servant   *n phr* (probably 20th century)   In a sadomasochistic scenario,* the submissive* in the role of a men-

ial servant, which role may include special dress as well as the performance of a variety of personal and household tasks for the dominant*   "Page servant needed to fulfill fantasy of cruel master with kind heart" (personal ad, adult bookstore, Columbus, Ohio, 4/14/87).

page service   *n phr* (probably 20th century)   Duties of a page servant*   "Is page service your fantasy? Call Lynn and let me satisfy you!" (personal ad, adult bookstore, Columbus, Ohio, 3/23/87).

pain   *n* (*OED* c. 1300)   Physical, mental, or emotional distress or suffering, and often the sadomasochistic activities associated with the production of such distress and suffering   "New to S/M scene, but into french and greek, some bondage, no pain" (personal ad, restroom wall, bar, Columbus, Ohio, 3/12/87).

panty fetish   *n phr* (see etym. note at fetish; probably 20th century)   Fetish involving (mostly women's) underwear   "Let me satisfy your panty fetish" (personal ad, adult bookstore, Columbus, Ohio, 4/3/87).

panty gag   *n phr* (probably 20th century)   Women's underwear used as a gag in the humiliation* of a panty slave*   "Taste my sweet cunny juices when I sit on your face, then savor my smells when I stuff a panty gag in your mouth" (personal ad, adult bookstore, Columbus, Ohio, 2/13/87).

panty slave   *n phr* (see etym. note at slave; probably 20th century)   Kind of slave,* one that suffers humiliation* through the use of (perhaps dirty) women's underwear; such humiliation may include binding and gagging with panties, wearing panties on the head, etc., and typically helps to satisfy a panty fetish*   "Panty slaves are fairly common, especially guys who get off on sticking dirty ones in their mouth" (personal interview, "Lucinda," 2/19/87). *See also* panty gag.

parachute ball collar   *n   phr* (probably 20th century)   Device used in sadomasochistic relationships to inflict pain on the submissive's* testicles; the parachute ball
collar consists of an adjustable leather ring—which is placed
around the scrotum above the testicles and tightened—onto
which is attached a length of cord or chain with a variably
weighted parachute at the end, which, when dropped from
varying heights and with varying amounts of weight attached, pulls on the collar and induces pain (*CBD*, p. 3).

party   *n* (Spears 20th century, 'group sex')   *See* Roman   "Bi-couple looking for others interested in parties"
(personal ad, adult bookstore, Columbus, Ohio, 2/22/87).
Also Roman arts, Roman culture.

passive   *n* (Spears lists *passive participant* 'catamite' as
current in homosexual usage in 20th century; probably 20th
century)   *See* masochist   "I have a few openings for
new passives, nothing very severe, just birching and chains"
(personal interview with "Lady in Black," 3/18/87). *Also* bottom, M (2), right hip pocket, S (3), slave, sub, submissive.

pb   *n phr* (probably 20th century)   *See* penis punishment   "I command you to call me if you need pb followed
by sucking, licking, and beating off!" (personal ad, restroom
wall, bar, Columbus, Ohio, 2/19/87). *pb* is an abbreviation
of penis bondage. *Also* penis bondage, penis torture, pp, pt.

peanut grinder   *n phr* (probably 20th century)   Device
used in sadomasochistic relationships to inflict pain on the
testicles of the masochist*; peanut grinders come in a variety
of styles, but have in common the characteristic of being able
to encase the testicles and exert pressure on them from all
sides (*CBD*, p. 4, ad for peanut grinders).

pee fun   *n phr* (Spears 19th century, *pee* 'urine'; probably
20th century)   *See* golden shower   "Also love Bi-love,
pee fun, and animal action" (*Intimate* 1, no. 1: 25, personal
ad). *Also* GS, G/S, G.S., pissing.

penis bondage   *n phr* (probably 20th century)   *See* penis punishment   As in "Cock and ball torture, penis bondage, showers of all kinds, animals you've never dreamed of, all in one torturing video" (information supplied by vice squad, Columbus Police Dept., 3/11/87). *Also* pb, penis torture, pp, pt.

penis punishment   *n   phr*   (probably   20th   century)   Sadomasochism involving torture* of the penis, which torture may include whipping, piercing, cockblocking,* stretching, crushing, etc.   "I believe in testicles [sic], penis punishment, catheters, enemas" (*B & D Pleasures* no. 56: 26, personal ad). *Also* pb, penis bondage, penis torture, pp, pt.

penis stock   *n phr* (probably 20th century)   Stock* made especially to hold and torture the submissive's* penis   "Bondage, spanking, penis stock, seduction in bondage are all good for me" (*Women in Command* no. 16: 25, personal ad).

penis torture   *n phr* (probably 20th century)   *See* penis punishment   "It is absolutely Sheer Torture to observe penis torture, flagellation and smothering administered by these 2 Superior Dominatrixes" (*Women in Command* no. 16: 23, videotape ad). *Also* pb, penis bondage, pp, pt.

pen pal   *n phr* (*W9* 1938, 'friend made and kept through written correspondence'; probably 20th century)   Partner in a sadomasochistic relationship that exists solely through written correspondence   "SWM looking for panty slave into french, greek—no pen pals, only the real thing!" (personal ad, adult bookstore, Columbus, Ohio, 4/15/87).

pet lover   *n phr* (see etym. note at pet; probably 20th century)   Sadomasochist especially interested in the use of pets in sadomasochistic scenarios*   "Pet lover has complete repertoire of furry creatures to share (no feathers yet)" (personal ad, adult bookstore, Columbus, Ohio, 1/27/87). *See also* canine interests.

pets *n pl* (*OED* 1539, *pet*; probably 20th century) Animals used in a sadomasochistic relationship, or bestiality* itself "I'm into it all, all cultures, bondage, discipline (all kinds), heavy S/M, fettishes [*sic*], fantasies, even pets" (personal ad, adult bookstore, Columbus, Ohio, 2/23/87). *See also* canine interests.

petticoat discipline *n phr* (see etym. note at discipline; probably 20th century) Form of discipline* and humiliation* in which a male submissive* is clad in women's lingerie and then made to endure various degrading actions by the (usually female) dominant,* which actions may include the dominant spitting, stepping, urinating, or defecating on the submissive "Total Petticoat discipline when mistress punishes her pantywaist sissy! This slave clad in women's lingerie is punished beneath the spikes and voluptuous body of his Goddess!" (*Women in Command* no. 16: 5, videotape ad). *Also* petticoat dressing, petticoat punishment.

petticoat dressing *n phr* (probably 20th century) *See* petticoat discipline "TVs especially wanted for petticoat dressing" (personal ad, adult bookstore, Columbus, Ohio, 1/23/87). *Also* petticoat punishment.

petticoat punishment *n phr* (see etym. note at punishment) *See* petticoat discipline "I love: fetish, leather, boots, heel- [*sic*], bondage, discipline, spanking, humiliation, mental/verbal/physical abuse, teasing/denial, footworship, equestrian, petticoat punishment" (*Bizarre Lifestyles* 1, no. 1: 41). *Also* petticoat dressing.

pickle *inter* (probably 20th century) *See* red (1) "Some say a specific word; *red* and *pickle* are real common, but it could be anything agreed on in advance by all the people involved" (personal interview, "Lucinda," 2/19/87).

pierce   *v* (*OED* 1297, 'puncture, make a hole in')   Use a sharp instrument to put a hole into the penis, testicles, nipples, or labia, usually of a masochist* *-ing*   *n*   (*OED* 1386, 'act of putting a hole in')   "I am into whipping, piercing, heavy cock and ball torture, and whatever else strikes my fancy at the moment" (*SM Express* no. 24: 12, personal ad).

pillory   *n* (*OED* 1189)   Device used in sadomasochistic relationships as a means of securing the head and arms of the masochist*; pillories are usually made of wood, perhaps pile-lined, and have holes through which the hands and head are placed (*B & D Pleasures* no. 56: 29, ad for pillories). *See also* stock.

pin prick C/R   *n phr* (probably 20th century)   *See* studded cockring (*The Underground*, ads for cockrings). *Also* English bracelet, English harness C/R, spike bracelet, studded bracelet.

piss club   *n phr* (probably 20th century)   Group of people, the members of which meet regularly for golden showers*   "Piss clubs are getting more and more common" (personal interview, "Lucinda," 2/19/87).

piss enema   *n phr* (see etym. notes at enema and pissing; probably 20th century)   Enema* that uses (usually human) urine instead of water or another substance   "Bi-Bitch nurse taking a few slaves to submit to total body worship, controlled body functions, piss enemas, more" (*B & D Pleasures* no. 56; personal ad).

pissing   *n*   (*OED*   1398, 'urination')   *See* golden shower   "If you're into B&D, punishment, pissing, send me $5 for great closeup photos" (personal ad, adult bookstore, Columbus, Ohio, 2/11/87). *Also* GS, G/S, G.S., pee fun.

play   1:   *n*   (*OED* 1200, 'amusement'; probably 20th century)   Participation in sadomasochistic scenario.*

2: *v* (*OED* 1391, 'amuse oneself through activity'; probably 20th century) Participate in sadomasochistic scenario "Submissive needs playmate for play" (personal ad, adult bookstore, Columbus, Ohio, 3/12/87).

playmate *n* (*OED* 1642, 'companion in play'; probably 20th century) Sadomasochist, usually one for hire "Playmate will satisfy all fantasies of weak but generous males and bis" (personal ad, adult bookstore, Columbus, Ohio, 2/19/87).

playroom *n* (*OED* 1819, 'rumpus room'; probably 20th century) *See* dungeon As in "Come into my playroom and enjoy the fruits of my labors!" (see Samois 1982, 252). *Also* mardi gras room, training room.

playtoy *n* (probably 20th century) Device used in a sadomasochistic scenario* "Mistress Dianne wants to meet you and has a fully equipped dungeon for your pleasure—all kinds of playtoys, etc." (personal ad, adult bookstore, Columbus, Ohio, 3/17/87).

pleasure restraint *n phr* (see etym. note at restraint; probably 20th century) **1:** Kind of restraint* used in bondage,* which restraint accomplishes its task without the extreme discomfort associated with traditional ropes, chains, and barbed wire; pleasure restraints include velvet ropes, pile-lined stocks, etc., and are most frequently used by those who practice light* (as opposed to heavy*) sadomasochism "Partner needed, M/F, for light bondage and discipline, pleasure restraints, no severe pain" (personal ad, adult bookstore, Columbus, Ohio, 1/29/87). **2:** Kind of restraint used in bondage, which restraint positions the submissive's* head so that pleasure to the dominant* is inevitable, as having the submissive's head strapped between the dominant's legs "The restraint went around the back of my head and her hips so that I was strapped into cunnilingus position. I could just maneuver my tongue; but it was impossible to recoil from this hairy forest nor to even turn my head away. It locked me right in place" (*Women in Command* no. 16: 4, col. 3).

plug   *v* (*OED* 1630, 'stop up a hole'; probably 20th century)   Insert a butt plug* into the submissive's* anus, usually for the purpose of preventing the expulsion of a forced enema*   *n*   (*OED* 1627, 'something used to stop up a hole, which it tightly fits'; probably 20th century)   *See* butt plug   **-ed**   (*OED* 1872, 'state or condition of being stopped up, as of a hole'; probably 20th century)   "Then they gave me another enema, plugged me and had me write to you" (*Corporal* 10, no. 3: 10, col. 3).

plug gag   *n* (see etym. note at gag; probably 20th century)   Kind of gag,* one which has a long protuberance that fits into the mouth, as in a cock mouth gag* (*CBD*, p. 7, ad for gags). *See also* cock mouth gag.

pony   *n*   (probably   20th   century)   *See*   pony slave   "SBF desires to act out the fantasy of being a MBM's pony" (personal ad, adult bookstore, Columbus, Ohio, 3/15/87).

pony boy   *n phr* (probably 20th century)   Male pony slave*   "Pony boys are pretty common; it's one of the best ways to humiliate most guys" (personal interview, "Lady in Black," 2/13/87). *See also* pony girl.

pony girl   *n phr* (probably 20th century)   Female pony slave*   "Dominant male, 30's, wishes to correspond and meet with anyone who is interested in pony girls. I have trained many submissive females in the art of being a pony girl. No fees" (*B & D Pleasures* no. 56: 20). *See also* pony boy.

pony slave   *n phr* (see etym. note at slave; probably 20th century)   Submissive* that is made to act like a horse through equestrian training*   "Pony slaves now being accepted, novices OK, I've trained many docile men and women" (personal ad, adult bookstore, Columbus, Ohio, 3/21/87). *Also* pony. *See also* pony boy, pony girl.

posing jock   *n phr* (*OED* 1922, *jock* 'athletic supporter'; probably 20th century)   Device used in sadomasochistic scenarios* as a means of framing the penis and making it look more alluring; posing jocks are constructed similarly to standard athletic supporters, though they are usually made of a soft leather, may be decorated with studs or small chains, and usually have adjustable leather laces (*CLBR*, p. 6, ad for posing jocks).

postal slave   *n phr* (probably 20th century)   Pen pal* that is a slave*   "Dominant, Kinky, Discreet, Bi-lady, late 40's, seeks female submissives who seek 'n need my strict guidance, humiliating degrading duties, punishments via mail as my personal postal slaves" (*Intimate* 1, no. 1: 31, personal ad).

pp   *n phr* (probably 20th century)   *See* penis punishment   "Mostly in public newspapers you'll find things like *pp, pt, nt, ff, tt*—you know, code words to keep the cops off their asses and so the newspaper'll print it" (personal interview, Briar Rose, S/M Women's Support Group, Columbus, Ohio, 3/19/87). *pp* is an abbreviation of penis punishment. *Also* pb, penis bondage, penis torture, pt.

princess   *n* (perhaps by analogy to queen; probably 20th century)   *See* masochist   "Dominant, 30, funloving, understanding, seeks beautiful, naughty Princess for loving relationship, incorporating sensible, erotic spanking" (*Corporal* 10, no. 3: 34, personal ad).

prolonged ritual   *n phr* (probably 20th century)   *See* protracted ritual   "Sissies, don't write! We're into heavy pain and prolonged rituals. If you're not serious, don't waste our time" (personal ad, adult bookstore, Columbus, Ohio, 2/28/87). *Also* extended ritual, prolonged scene.

prolonged scene   *n phr* (probably 20th century)   *See* protracted ritual   "Interests include bondage, humiliation, prolonged scenes and more" (*SM Express* no. 24: 20, personal ad). *Also* extended ritual, prolonged ritual.

protracted ritual   *n phr* (probably 20th century) Especially long sadomasochistic scenario.* See citation at anal rape. *Also* extended ritual, prolonged ritual, prolonged scene.

pt   *n phr* (probably 20th century)   *See* penis punishment. See citation at nt. *pt* is an abbreviation of penis torture, and occasionally occurs as *PT*. *Also* pb, penis bondage, penis torture, pp.

punish   *v* (*OED* 1812, 'censure, usually physically')   In a sadomasochistic scenario,* inflict verbal, emotional, and/or physical pain on the submissive*; punishment can assume a variety of forms, including torture, servitude, etc. **-ment**   *n*   (*OED* 1856, 'usually physical censurement'; probably 20th century)   Punishing activities as described in sense 1   "I'll tease, punish, delight you" (personal ad, adult bookstore, Columbus, Ohio, 2/25/87).

punishment helmet   *n phr* (probably 20th century)   *See* punishment hood   "Beautiful slave girls bound in leather, ropes and chains, and made to endure breast torture, tickling, punishment helmets and chastity belts" (*B & D Pleasures* no. 56: 22, videotape ad).

punishment hood   *n phr* (probably 20th century) Kind of hood,* one worn by submissive* in a sadomasochistic relationship as a means of discipline* or punishment*; punishment hoods are usually made of leather and may have studs on the inside or outside, either for decoration or for purposes of torture (*CBD*, p. 6, ad for punishment hoods). *Also* punishment helmet.

push the limits   *v phr* (probably 20th century)   Violate the original, preset limits of pain in a sadomasochistic scenario* in an acceptable way; typically the dominant* escalates the limits of pain to match the increasing intensity of the submissive's* sexual response, and this escalation continues until a negative reaction occurs from the submissive **-ing the limits** *n phr* (probably 20th century) Violation of the original, preset limits of pain in a sadomasochistic scenario, as explained in sense 1 "Submissive enjoys all cultures, B & D, pushing the limits" (personal ad, adult bookstore, Columbus, Ohio, 4/12/87).

queen *n* (*OED* 825, 'woman who is chief ruler of a state'; probably 20th century) *See* dominatrix As in "She is his queen and the queen of all torture!" (see "Exquisite Agony," videotape). *Also* amazon (2), bitch goddess, discipliness, dominant bitch, dominatrix bitch, female dominant, femdom, goddess, headmistress, mastix, mistress.

queening *n* (probably 20th century) *See* heavy squatting "I am a submissive slave, 22, 37–24–36, who will do your every bidding. I'm especially into queening—I want your ass on my face!" (personal ad, adult bookstore, Columbus, Ohio, 2/22/87). *Also* face-sitting.

rabbit fur *n phr* (probably 20th century) Kind of mitten,* one usually made of rabbit fur and used to soothe a freshly flagellated buttock "Rabbit furs don't really do anything besides make the person temporarily feel less pain" (personal interview, "Lucinda," 2/19/87).

rack *n* (*OED* 1305) Iron bar or framework to which masochists* can be secured for further punishment* (*CBD*, p. 8, ad for racks). *See also* finger rack.

ram *v* (OED 1519, 'force or drive down or in by heavy blows'; Spears 16th century, 'copulation'; Spears 19th century, 'copulation with a female') Perform forced

Greek*   **-ing**   *n* (*OED* 1854, 'action of thrusting down or in by blows') *See* forced Greek   "She had me get completely undressed, I mean totally nude, and she stretched me out over the horse. My feet were tied to the legs of the horse so that I was wide open from the rear. She then put on her strap-on dildo. I mean this is a monster thing. It must be ten inches long, and after the head, which is circumcised, it is very thin, but it gradually grows to a giant thickness. MISTRESS LIZ is about five-foot-eight, and weighs about 135, so her ramming into you is not a little thing, you feel it, and I did, practically screaming in horror" (*Corporal* 10, no. 3: 4, col. 3).

real   *adj*   (*OED*   1559,   'genuine,   unadulterated') Complete; full; genuine; undiminished and unadulterated. See citations at real masochism and real sadism. Used only in combination, as in real pain, etc. *Also true.*

real masochism   *n phr* (see etym. notes at real and masochism; probably 20th century)   Masochism* that is real*; heavy* masochism   **-ist**   *n phr* (see etym. notes at real and masochist; probably 20th century)   Masochist* that is real; masochist who does only heavy masochism   "Bi-couple into real masochism ONLY—no TVs or kinks, no pen pals, no light S/M" (personal ad, adult bookstore, Columbus, Ohio, 3/12/87). *Also* true masochism, -ist.

real sadism   *n phr* (see etym. notes at real and sadism; probably 20th century)   Sadism* that is real*; heavy masochism   **-ist**   *n phr*   (see etym. notes at real and masochist; probably 20th century)   Sadist* that is real; sadist who does only heavy sadism   "Real sadist needs to meet REAL masochist, someone who can satisfy my need for power and pain—no pen pals, etc." (personal ad, adult bookstore, Columbus, Ohio, 1/29/87). *Also* true sadism, true sadist.

red   **1:** *inter*   (probably 20th century)   Universal safe word* meaning 'stop; I've had enough' (information provided by Draya Love, a B & D lesbian, "Women on Sex: B & D," Playboy Channel, 3/8/87). *Also* pickle. *See also* green, yellow. **2:** *adj* (probably 20th century) Open to fistfucking* "GWM—20, 5'6", red/blue, seeks leatherman to 30 to initiate me into the leather scene" (*GT* 3, no. 9: 20, personal ad). *See also* red handkerchief.

red handkerchief *n phr* (probably 20th century) Sadomasochist who especially likes fistfucking* or scenarios* containing fistfucking "Two red handkerchiefs are better than one" (personal ad, bar, restroom wall, Columbus, Ohio, 2/24/87). In an S & M bar, a person wearing a red handkerchief is advertising for someone with whom to participate in fistfucking.

refined *adj* (*OED* 1668) Raised to a high degree of expertise and precision "Refined sadist desirous of making the acquaintance of masochistic partners for ongoing relationship" (personal ad, adult bookstore, Columbus, Ohio, 1/30/87).

restrain *v* (*OED* c. 1340, 'limit; inhibit'; probably 20th century) In bondage,* restrict a person's movement as described under restraint* "Letting someone restrain you is an extremely common kind of fantasy; it ranks right up there with rape" (personal interview, "Lucinda," 2/19/87).

restraint *n* (*OED* c. 1400, 'something that limits or inhibits'; probably 20th century) Something used in bondage* to restrict a person's movement, as straps, chains, ropes, barbed wire, handcuffs, etc. "We carry a full line of restraints and torture devices" (ad, adult bookstore, Columbus, Ohio, 3/14/87).

restraint mask *n phr* (see etym. note at mask; probably 20th century) Kind of mask,* one specifically designed to exert pressure on the face of the wearer (*CBD*, p. 6, ad for restraint masks).

restrict   *v* (*OED* 1824, 'tie up; confine by tying'; probably 20th century)   In a sadomasochistic scenario,* confine in any way, as through tying, hobbling, cuffing, etc., usually for the purposes of bondage* and discipline* **-ion**   (*OED* 1758, 'confinement'; probably 20th century)   In a sadomasochistic scenario, confinement of any sort, as described in sense 1, or anything used to achieve such confinement   "Restrict your partner using our newest playtoys" (*CBD*, p. 2, ad).

reward   1:   *n*   (*OED* 14th century, 'return for hardship endured'; probably 20th century)   *See* rewards of worship. **2:**   *v*   (*OED* c. 1350, 'repay for merit'; probably 20th century)   Give rewards of worship*   "Serve me, then grovel, and maybe I'll reward you by letting you lick my asshole" (personal ad, adult bookstore, Columbus, Ohio, 2/22/87).

rewards of worship   *n phr* (probably 20th century) Re ward given to a slave* by his or her master* for especially obedient behavior; typically the rewards include oral adoration* (of the master) or some special kind of torture (of the slave)   "Rewards of worship allowed for those of you who are worthy" (*Women in Command* no. 16: 25, personal ad). *Also* reward (1).

rightful   place   *n   phr*   (probably   20th   century)   Scenario* of exaggerated humiliation.* See citation at mature.

right   hip   pocket   *n   phr* (probably 20th century) Slave*   "*Right hip pocket* means the submissive, the slave, but it's more used in wearing hankies than anything else" (personal interview, "Lucinda," 2/19/87). In an S & M bar, a handkerchief worn in the right hip pocket advertises that the wearer is a slave in sadomasochistic relationships. *Also* bottom, M (2), masochist, passive, S (3), sub, submissive. *See also* left hip pocket.

rim   *v* (Spears 20th century)   Do anilingus* and/or Greek*   **-ing**   *n*   (Spears 20th century)   Act of anilingus or Greek   "Mistress Vicki has a few openings for submissive males whose interests include showers, scat, rimming and kissing my beautiful cunt" (*Intimate* 1, no. 1: 20, personal ad).

rodent route   *v* (*W9* 1859, n, *rodent* 'kind of small mammal'; probably 20th century)   Insert a small rodent—minus claws and teeth—into the anus of a masochist* and allow it to squirm and wiggle until it (i.e., the rodent) dies, after which it is removed   **-ing**   *n phr*   (probably 20th century)   Activity described in sense 1   "Heavy S & M, pets okay, no rodent routing" (personal ad, restroom wall, OSU main library, 3/11/87). *See also* gerbil, gerbiling.

role   *n* (*OED* 1606, 'character or role played by an actor'; probably 20th century)   Character or part played by a sadomasochist in a scenario*   "Roles are almost always decided in advance, just so there are no surprises for the submissive" (personal interview, "Lucinda," 2/19/87).

role play   *v* (*W9* 1949, 'act out'; probably 20th century)   Act out various sadomasochistic fantasies, including domination,* various fetishes,* the arts,* etc.   **-ing**   *n phr*   (probably 20th century)   Acting out of fantasies in a sadomasochistic relationship, as described in sense 1   "Young, very attractive, nicely-built, normal, healthy, sincere 24 year old white male, college student from extremely nice family seeks one truly sincere female/couple/TV any age, with similar interest in role playing, dressing up, and acting out their favorite dominant and submissive fantasies, especially ones giving or receiving good, old-fashioned, bare-bottom spankings, in a safe, playful, enjoyable fun way" (*Corporal* 10, no. 3: 33, personal ad).

role set   *n phr* (see etym. note at role; probably 20th century)   Pair of characters agreed to be role-played by a dominant* and submissive* in a scenario*; such pairs typically include teacher/student, kidnapper/victim, rapist/victim, master/slave, and guardian/child.   "Imaginative master now accepting new slaves for all role sets" (personal ad, adult bookstore, Columbus, Ohio, 2/22/87).

Roman   *n* (probably 20th century)   Sadomasochistic scenarios* including three or more participants; orgiastic sadomasochism   "SWM into all cultures, including Roman, wants to meet SBF or TV who can teach me the ways of the world" (personal ad, adult bookstore, Columbus, Ohio, 3/17/87). Often appears uncapitalized. *Also* party, Roman arts, Roman culture.

Roman arts   *n phr* (probably 20th century)   *See* Roman   "Stuffy CPA wishes to be instructed in the roman arts" (personal ad, adult bookstore, Columbus, Ohio, 1/19/87). *Also* party, Roman culture.

Roman culture   *n phr* (probably 20th century)   *See* Roman   "Roman culture is the one most often talked about but least often practiced" (personal interview, "Lucinda," 2/19/87). *Also* party, Roman arts.

rubber band torture   *n phr* (*W9* 1895, *rubber band*; probably 20th century)   In a sadomasochistic scenario,* any of a number of specialized tortures using rubber bands   "She is subjected to rubber band torture" (*SM Express* no. 24: 8, videotape ad).

rubber cockring   *n phr* (probably 20th century)   Kind of cockring,* one specifically made of rubber and designed to expand somewhat with enlargement of the penis (*CBD*, p. 4, ad for rubber cockrings).

S   *n* (probably 20th century)   **1:** *See* sadism   "Interested in S but don't know where to turn?" (personal ad, restroom wall, bar, Columbus, Ohio, 2/14/87). **2:** *See* sadist   "I'm an S without an M" (personal ad, restroom wall, bar, Columbus, Ohio, 3/23/87). *Also* corporalist, dom, dominant, left hip pocket, M (3), master, sender, sir, taskmaster, top. **3:** *See* slave, submissive As in "I want to lick your feet and be your S." *Also* bottom, M (2), masochist, passive, right hip pocket, sub. (The second definition is common everywhere except the West Coast; the third definition prevails only on the West Coast. See note 5 in the prefatory matter to the glossary.)

sadism *n* (*OED* 1888) Sexual orientation in which one connects the giving of physical and/or psychological pain or discomfort with sexual pleasure "Sadism is more prevalent than any non-participant knows or wants to know" (personal interview, "Lucinda," 2/19/87). *Also* S (1).
-ist *n* (*OED* 1897) In a sadomasochist relationship, the dominant partner; the one who binds, whips, abuses, humiliates, and otherwise punishes the masochist* As in "It's hard to say whether there are more sadists or masochists out there; a lot of people really get off on being dominated, but a lot of people enjoy giving pain, too" (personal interview, "Lady in Black," 3/18/87). *Also* corporalist, dom, dominant, left hip pocket, M (3), master, S (2), sender, sir, taskmaster, top.

sadomasochism *n* (*W9* 1922) Connection of the giving and receiving of psychological and/or physical discomfort or pain with sexual pleasure; in each sadomasochistic relationship there is typically at least one sadist* and one masochist*; sadomasochism is typically seen as a more forceful and intense form of bondage and discipline* by members of the subculture (see especially Weinberg and Kamel 1983). *Also* S and M, SM, S/M, S-M, S.M., Spaghetti and Macaroni.
-ist *n* (20th century) One who participates in sadomasochism "What's a sadomasochist? There's a little bit of that in all of us, honey" (personal interview, "Lady in Black," 3/18/87). *See also* sexually otherwise, sexual variants.

safe *adj* (*OED* c. 1290, 'in sound health; well;

whole') *See* clean   "Safe males and bis only need apply" (personal ad, adult bookstore, Columbus, Ohio, 3/26/87).

safe fun   *n phr* (probably 20th century)   Observance of a masochist's* limits to pain by a sadist*   "GWM—44, dominant, seeks macho type under 40 for safe fun" (*GT* 3, no. 9: 20 personal ad).

safe   sex   *n   phr*   (probably   20th   century) Sadomasochistic scenario* in which there is no exchange of bodily fluids   "Male dominant, 42, interested in scenes of safe sex only" (personal ad, adult bookstore, Columbus, Ohio, 4/30/87).

safe word   *n phr* (probably 20th century)   Word which, when uttered by the masochist* during a sadomasochistic scenario,* lets the sadist* know that the masochist has reached his or her limits of pain or believes that things are generally   getting   out   of   hand   and   wants   to stop   "Everybody into heavy S and M has a safe word. You have to. Even then it doesn't always stop things from going too far" (personal interview, "Lucinda," 2/19/87). *Also* key-word.

S and M   *n phr* (probably 20th century)   *See* sado-masochism   "Into S and M, light B and D, most fetishes and fantasies" (personal ad, adult bookstore, Columbus, Ohio, 1/31/87). *Also* SM, S/M, S-M, S.M., Spaghetti and Macaroni.

scat   *n*   (*W9*,   1927,   'excrement')   *See*   brown shower   As in "Interested in water sports, scat, and bond-age—no pain" (information supplied by Califia 1980, 136). *Also* Boston tea party, BS, B/S, hot turds.

scat club   *n phr* (probably 20th century)   Groups of people, the members of which meet regularly to share brown showers*   As in "Scat clubs are growing more and more common as their members continue to come out of the closet" (see Weinberg 1983, 381).

scenario   *n* (*OED* 1880, 'script of events'; probably 20th century)   In a sadomasochistic encounter, script of events or activities previously negotiated and agreed upon and then followed by all participants   "Scenarios are usually worked out right down to the finest detail. I mean, they have to be. There are a lot of crazies out there, you know" (personal interview, "Lucinda," 2/19/87). *Also* scene, script.

scene   *n* (*OED* 1594, 'script of events')   *See* scenario   "*Scene*? Sure, sometimes we use that word. It's the same as *scenario*; it just means what's going down, that's all" (personal interview, "Lady in Black," 3/18/87). *Also* script.

scissor   *v* (*OED* 1612, 'cut with scissors'; probably 20th century)   Wrap one's legs around another person who is on hands and knees and ride the person like a horse   **-ing**   *n*   (probably 20th century)   Act of using the legs as described in sense 1   "I used my legs to scissor her into submission" (*Corporal* 10, no. 3: 6, col. 1).

script   *n* (*OED* 1897, 'manuscript'; probably 20th century)   *See* scenario   "Dominant male, into heavy S and M, follows all scripts and promises disgression [*sic*] (personal ad, restroom wall, bar, Columbus, Ohio, 1/18/87). *Also* scene.

sender   *n* (*OED* c. 1200, 'one who sends something'; probably 20th century)   Sadist*   As in "Experienced sender requires YOU slut slave to call her!" (see Samois 1982, 31). *Also* corporalist, dom, dominant, left hip pocket, M (3), master, S (2), sir, taskmaster, top.

servant   *n* (*OED* 1433, 'one who is under the obligation to render certain services to, and to obey the orders of, a person'; probably 20th century)   Kind of maid,* one which does whatever the master* orders. See citation at maid.

serve   υ (*OED* 1382, 'be a slave, be in bondage')   Of a masochist,* be a slave* to and worship a sadist* with obedience   "The Submissive Life—Do you want to serve—permanently?" (*Corporal* 10, no. 33: personal ad).

service   **1:**   υ   (*OED* c. 1200, 'perform the duties of a servant'; probably 20th century)   Of a submissive,* do whatever his or her dominant* requires for sexual gratification   "Service your stud master's body, slut. Wash it with your bitch tongue! Do it!" (*Expose!*, pp. 151–52). **2:**   n   (*OED* 1469, 'work of a servant'; probably 20th century)   In a sadomasochistic scenario,* whatever is necessary for the sexual gratification of the dominant   "Her royal highness the queen bitch is now accepting into her service only the choicest of slut slaves" (personal ad, adult bookstore, Columbus, Ohio, 2/22/87). *See also* servitude.

servitude   n (*OED* 1471, 'condition of being a slave or a serf')   In a sadomasochistic scenario,* the complete bidding of a dominant*   "Personable, abjectly-humble, submissive male, 35, seeks sound, bare-bottom spankings, domestic servitude and forced body worship under the absolute mastership of a husky, strap-wielding, dominant woman, any age or color, residing East Central New England" (*Corporal* 10, no. 3: 35, personal ad). *See also* service.

sextrain, -ing   υ, n   (see etym. note at train)   *See* train, training   "I need an understanding woman to guide, sextrain, enslave me" (*Women in Command* no. 16: 25, personal ad). *Sextraining* also = obedience training.*

sexually   otherwise   *adj*   (probably   20th   century)   Sadomasochistic;   interested   in   sadomasochism   "Sexually otherwise male, 29, 6', 185, would like to meet female of same persuasion" (personal ad, restroom wall, bar, Columbus, Ohio, 2/19/87).

sexual   variants   n   *phr*   (probably   20th century)   Sadomasochistic activities, usually of a light* nature "Bored with the usual, the mundane, the every-day? Call Joan and let me introduce you to the world of sexual variants—experience pain and pleasure like you've never imagined" (personal ad, adult bookstore, Columbus, Ohio, 2/19/87).

shame **1:** *n* (*OED* c. 725) Painful emotion caused by disgrace, unworthiness, ridicule, etc. **2:** *v* (*OED* c. 897) Cause a painful emotion as described in sense 1 "This bitch can shame you into doing anything to serve her" (personal ad, adult bookstore, Columbus, Ohio, 4/14/87).

she-male **1:** *n* (probably 20th century) Transvestite who routinely wears female clothing conspicu-ously in public and is, to all outward appearances, completely indistinguishable from a woman; man who practices cross-dressing* "SWM wants to meet future live-in slave, male, bi, TV, she-males only, no females" (personal ad, adult book-store, Columbus, Ohio, 3/30/87). **2:** *n* (probably 20th century) Hermaphrodite or partial transsexual, usually one with female breasts and male reproductive organs "I want your meat and your boobs, she-males" (personal ad, restroom wall, bar, Columbus, Ohio, 1/14/87). *Also* bull bitch. **3:** *adj* (probably 20th century) Pertaining to behavior typical of a transvestite as described in sense 1 "I'm no psychologist, but I think there are transvestite and she-male tendencies in most men" (personal interview, "Lucinda," 2/19/87). **4:** *adj* (probably 20th cen-tury) Pertaining to behavior typical of a hermaphrodite or transsexual as described in sense 2 "STUFF ME WITH YOUR SHE-MALE MEAT" (title, *Bizarre* no. 84: 3).

shit blister **1:** *v* (probably 20th century) Intro-duce small amounts of feces subcutaneously in a submis-sive,* usually through grinding or paddling. **2:** *n* (probably 20th century) Small amounts of feces intro-duced subcutaneously in a submissive as described in sense

1   "I have shit blistered them. To put it concisely, I have introduced small amounts of my soft brown excrement subcutaneously all over their genitals and faces" (*Club*, "Holiday Special," 1976, p. 78, letter column).

shock box   *n phr* (probably 20th century)   Battery-operated device used in sadomasochism, which device has four electrodes, one each of which is placed in the anus, in the vagina or around the penis, and on each nipple of the masochist*; the shock box then gives electrical shocks of varying intensity and duration, usually within certain preset limits and at the whim of the sadist (*SM Express*, no. 24: 8, ad for shock boxes). *See also* electric zapper.

shower   *n* (probably 20th century)   Golden shower* or brown shower*   See citation at rimming.

sincere   *adj* (probably 20th century)   Willing to pay for sadomasochistic services; generous*   "Sincere men only need apply" (personal ad, adult bookstore, Columbus, Ohio, 3/23/87).   **-ity**   *n*   (probably 20th century) Payment for sadomasochistic services   "Your sincerity will be greatly appreciated" (personal ad, adult bookstore, Columbus, Ohio, 2/19/87). *See also* generosity.

sir   *n*   (probably   20th   century)   *See*   sadist   "Submissive male needs sir" (personal ad, adult bookstore, Columbus, Ohio, 2/21/87). *Also* corporalist, dom, dominant, left hip pocket, M (3), master, S (2), sender, taskmaster, top.

slave   **1:**   *v*   (*OED* 1729, 'toil or work as a slave'; probably 20th century)   Act as submissive* or masochist* in a sadomasochistic relationship. **2:**   *n*   (*OED* 1559, 'one who is completely under the domination of a specified influence'; probably 20th century)   Submissive or masochist in a sadomasochistic relationship, especially one who undergoes extreme pain or torment   "Will accept new submissive and educated mature slaves for personal servitude and strict training" (*Bizarre Lifestyles* 1, no 1: 45, personal ad). *Also* bottom, M (2), masochist, passive, right hip pocket, S (3), sub, submissive. **-ry** *n* (*OED* 1604, 'condition of a slave'; probably 20th century) Condition of being a slave as described in sense 2 "Enjoy slavery, fetishes, fantasies of all kinds" (personal ad, adult bookstore, Columbus, Ohio, 3/27/87).

slave exchange *n phr* (see etym. note at slave; probably 20th century) Trading of slaves* between their masters,* which trading must be an agreed-upon part of the scenario* "Live-in possible. Also Mistresses, B&D couples for parties, slave exchanges" (*B & D Pleasures* no. 56: 20, personal ad). *Also* time buying, trading.

slave princess *n phr* (see etym. note at slave; probably 20th century) Slave* who is female and especially young and pretty "Would you like to be the slave princess of Bad Bart? Do you qualify?" (personal ad, adult bookstore, Columbus, Ohio, 2/22/87).

sling *n* (*OED* 1323–24, 'device used to raise and lower bulky objects'; probably 20th century) Device used to raise and lower or to suspend submissives* during a sadomasochistic scenario,* as during fistfucking* (*CBD*, p. 11, ad for slings).

slut **1:** *n* (*OED* 1450, 'woman of low or loose moral character'; Spears mid–20th century, homosexual use, 'promiscuous homosexual'; probably 20th century) Lowly, worthless person "Hey, you slut! Contact me NOW" (personal ad, adult bookstore, Columbus, Ohio, 4/11/87). **2:** *adj* (probably 20th century) Pertaining to a lowly, worthless person "Dominant goddess looking for new slut slave to worship my hot black feet" (personal ad, adult bookstore, Columbus, Ohio, 3/11/87). *Slut* is used primarily as a means of humiliation,* and appears frequently in personal ads as a means of enticement.

SM   *n* (see etym. note at sadomasochism; probably 20th century)   *See* sadomasochism   "Black momma into SM, B & D, french, greek, golden and brown showers, fantasies, all but pain" (personal ad, adult bookstore, Columbus, Ohio, 2/18/87). *Also* S and M, S/M, S-M, S.M., Spaghetti and Macaroni.

S/M   *n* (see etym. note at sadomasochism; probably 20th century)   *See* sadomasochism   "Is B/D, S/M your thing?" (personal ad, adult bookstore, Columbus, Ohio, 1/31/87) *Also* S and M, SM, S-M, S.M., Spaghetti and Macaroni.

S.M.   *n* (see etym. note at sadomasochism; probably 20th century)   *See* sadomasochism   "I like all S-M but heavy pain" (personal ad, adult bookstore, Columbus, Ohio, 3/23/87). *Also* S and M, SM, S/M, S.M., Spaghetti and Macaroni.

S.M.   *n* (see etym. note at sadomasochism; probably 20th century)   *See* sadomasochism   "White babe, 23, 42DD–23–35, into it all, even S.M., for the right sincere man" (personal ad, adult bookstore, Columbus, Ohio, 3/29/87). *Also* S and M, SM, S/M, S-M, Spaghetti and Macaroni.

SM & M   *n phr* (probably 20th century)   Sexual mastery and masochism   "SWM looking for SM & M" (personal ad, adult bookstore, Columbus, Ohio, 3/2/87).

smother   **1:**   *n*   (*OED* 1548, 'suffocate by the prevention of breathing'; probably 20th century)   Role play* in such a way that the dominant* pretends to suffocate the submissive,* as through the use of a cock mouth gag,* a pair of underwear stuffed in the mouth, constriction of the neck with ropes, etc. **2:**   *n*   (*OED* 1602, 'act of suffocation through prevention of breathing'; probably 20th century) Role playing as described in sense 1   "She then smothers him and forces him to service her through panty smothering" (*Women in Command* no. 16: 14, videotape ad).

smother panties   *n phr* (see etym. note at smother; probably 20th century)   Kind of women's underwear made specifically for the fantasy of smothering*; the underwear may be made of a special material, such as satin, may be specially scented, as with feces or urine, and may have a special strap that fits around the back of the head to prevent it from being spit out of the mouth   "Complete line of fetish and fantasy items—gags, chains, whips, smother panties, gates of hell, etc." (ad, adult bookstore, Columbus, Ohio, 3/11/87).

snuff movie   *n phr* (20th century)   Pornographic film in which sexual excitement is linked to someone's (usually torturous) death; snuff movies are hard to locate because so few have been made (due to actual deaths occurring in their making)   "Yeah, you don't see many of them snuff movies, only one I think I've ever seen" (personal interview, "Lucinda," 2/19/87).

social   *n* (*OED* 1876, 'social gathering or party'; probably 20th century)   Meeting between two potential sadomasochistic partners for the purpose of becoming acquainted, sharing fantasies, discussing possible future scenarios,* etc.   "First meeting by mail, then a social in a public place, then we go to it" (personal ad, adult bookstore, Columbus, Ohio, 4/15/87).

solo   *n* (*OED* 1712, 'alone; without a companion or partner')   Sadomasochistic scenario* involving only one person; sadomasochism done to oneself   "I honor all desires—all fantasies, all fetishes, all toys, even solos" (personal ad, adult bookstore, Columbus, Ohio, 2/2/87).

Spaghetti and Macaroni   *n phr* (probably 20th century) Code phrase often used on the signs advertising S and M bars and restaurants; the bars typically serve neither spaghetti nor macaroni, but are signalling the knowing public of the sadomasochistic availability of many of the establishment's regular patrons. *Also* sadomasochism, S and M, SM, S/M, S-M, S.M. *See also* Burgers and Dogs.

Spanish   *n* (probably 20th century)   Sadomasochistic scenario* especially characterized by large amounts of verbal abuse   "I'm REALLY into Spanish, so lash out at me with your velvet tongue" (personal ad, adult bookstore, Columbus, Ohio, 1/29/87). Rare.

spank   1:   *v* (*OED* 1727)   Flagellate a person's buttocks, as with the bare hand, a spanking glove,* etc.   **2:**   *n*   (*OED* 1785)   Flagellation of the buttocks as described in sense 1   **-ing**   *n*   (*OED* 1854)   Flagellation of the buttocks as described in sense 1   "My imagination and expertise in humiliation, slave training, spanking TV discipline [*sic*] are unsurpassed" (*Bizarre Lifestyles* 1, no. 1: 55, personal ad).

spanking glove   *n phr* (*OED* 1854, *spanking*, *n*; *OED* c. 1000, *glove*, *n*; probably 20th century)   Kind of glove used for spanking in sadomasochistic relationships, which glove is typically made of leather and has metal studs on the palm (*CBD*, p. 2, ad for spanking gloves).

spike action   *n phr* (probably 20th century)   *See* trampling   "I yearn for your discipline, esp. spike action and licking the bottoms of your shoes" (personal ad, adult bookstore, Columbus, Ohio, 3/22/87). *Also* high heel discipline, high heel training.

spike bracelet   *n phr* (probably 20th century)   *See* studded cockring   (*The Underground*, ads for cockrings) *Also* English bracelet, English harness C/R, pin prick C/R, studded bracelet.

stable   *n* (Spears early 20th century, 'pimp's collection of prostitutes'; probably 20th century)   Sadist's* collection of masochists*   "Male slaves invited to apply for position in my stable" (*Bizarre Lifestyles* 1, no. 1: 46, personal ad).

stewardess   *n* (probably 20th century)   Female sadomasochist who is willing to travel to meet new partners "Stewardess typically flies the eastern states, can arrange schedule to suit yours" (personal ad, adult bookstore, Columbus, Ohio, 3/19/87).

stock   *n* (*OED* 1325)   Device used in sadomasochistic relationships to secure the feet and ankles—and occasionally the head and arms—of the submissive*; stocks are typically made of wood, may be pile-lined, and have holes through which the feet protrude (*B & D Pleasures* no. 56: 29, ad for stocks). *See also* pillory.

stocking bondage   *n phr* (see etym. note at bondage; probably 20th century)   Form of cock and ball torture* or breast torture* in which stockings are used to tie up and constrict the various parts of the body   "I produced a well-worn stocking from my purse and proceeded to tie his cock and balls tightly with it. First one know [*sic*] under his balls, and the other around the base of his cock.... I must have done this for an hour or more and, each time he tried to shoot, I tightened the stocking bondage" (*Corporal* 10, no. 3: 11, cols. 1–2; see also photo, col. 3).

story of "O"   *n phr* (20th century)   Sadomasochistic lifestyle characterized especially by spanking, whipping, forced Greek,* and perhaps the piercing of the masochist's* labia   "Willing to live Story of 'O', accept piercing tattooes, wish service in French, Greek"   (*Corporal* 10, no. 3: 37 personal ad). *The Story of "O"* is the title of a sadomasochistic novel ("O" being the female protagonist, a masochist) by Pauline Reage (a pseudonym) originally published in France in 1954 and subsequently translated and reprinted in the United States by Grove Press (New York, 1965).

str   *n, adj* (see etym. note at straight; probably 20th century)   *See* straight   "We like French and Str." (*Intimate* 1, no. 1: 23, personal ad). Also occasionally occurs as *str*.

straight   **1:**   *adj* (*OED* 1530, 'free from crookedness in conduct'; probably 20th century)   Pertaining to nonsa-

domasochist   or   nonsadomasochistic   activity.
2:   *n*   (probably 20th century)   Nonsadomasochist   "SWM, straight to date, seeks greek tutor for intensive
training" (personal ad, adult bookstore, Columbus, Ohio, 4/
14/87). *Also* str.

studded bracelet   *n phr* (probably 20th century)   *See*
studded cockring (*The Underground*, ads for cockrings).

studded cockring   *n phr* (probably 20th century)   Kind
of cockring,* one which has small studs or spikes on the
inner circumference, the purpose of which is to pierce the
skin of the penis and thus cause greater pain than that provided by ordinary cockrings (*The Underground*, ads for
cockrings). *Also* English bracelet, English harness bracelet,
English harness C/R, pin prick C/R, spike bracelet, studded
bracelet.

sub   *n* (probably 20th century)   *See* submissive   "I
am the perfect sub, use me for your pleasure and then cast
me aside!" (personal ad, adult bookstore, Columbus, Ohio,
4/12/87). *Also* bottom, M (2), masochist, passive, right hip
pocket, S (3), slave.

subjugate   *v* (*OED* 1589 'conquer, subdue')   Bring under complete physical or psychological control, within the
bounds of the sadomasochistic scenario*   **subjugation**
    n   (*OED* 1658, 'act of conquering') Complete physical
or psychological control, as described in sense 1   "She
beats, humiliates, and trains one of her clints [*sic*] as her
dog 'Mutt' through subjegation [*sic*]" (*Women in Command*
no. 16: 20, videotape ad). Frequently misspelled *subjegation*.

submissive   *n* (probably 20th century)   Masochist* or
slave* in a sadomasochistic relationship   "Let me be your
submissive, I need toilet training and general discipline"
(personal ad, adult bookstore, Columbus, Ohio, 4/4/87). *Also*
bottom, M (2), passive, right hip pocket, S (3), sub.

submit   *v* (*OED* c. 1374, 'give in to the wishes of another'; probably 20th century)   Of a masochist,* give in to the wishes of a sadist* within a sadomasochistic scenario*   **submission**   *n* (*OED* 1449, 'the condition of giving in to another; probably 20th century)   Giving in of a masochist to a sadist, as described in sense 1   "My slaves offer absolute submission or nothing—and I never settle for nothing!" (personal ad, adult bookstore, Columbus, Ohio, 2/27/87).

subservient   *adj* (*OED* 1647, 'subordinant in capacity or function'; probably 20th century)   Excessively submissive* and obsequious, usually to the point of being a total slave*   "I subserviently suckled each of his hard brown paps, and he grunted in bestial satisfaction, guiding my face across his upper body. He lifted one arm and roughly shoved my face beneath it" (*Expose!*, p. 36).

suffocate   *v* (*OED* 1599, 'kill by restricting the supply of air to the lungs'; probably 20th century)   In a sadomasochistic scenario* prevent or pretend to prevent someone from breathing as though to kill him or her   **-ion**   *n* (*OED* 1577, 'act of killing by restricting the supply of air to the lungs'; probably 20th century)   Act of suffocating as described in sense 1   "Suffocation is my special fantasy; what's yours?" (personal ad, adult bookstore, Columbus, Ohio, 2/12/87).

suspend   *v* (*OED* c. 1440, 'hang so as to allow free movement'; probably 20th century)   In a sadomasochistic scenario,* hang the submissive,* usually so as to render him or her powerless; submissives are most often suspended by their limbs or torso, but also occasionally by their necks   **-sion**   (*OED* 1546, 'act of hanging so as to allow free movement'; probably 20th century)   Hanging of a submissive as described in sense 1   "Suspension is my speciality" (personal ad, adult bookstore, Columbus, Ohio, 4/19/87); see also *B & D Pleasures* no. 56: 32, picture.

swing   *v* (Spears mid–20th century, 'be involved in sexual fads, group sex'; probably 20th century)   Participate in Roman* **swinging**   *n*   (probably   20th   century) "We're both into swinging" (personal ad, adult bookstore, Columbus, Ohio, 3/23/87).

switch   1:   *v* (probably 20th century)   Play the role of either the sadist* or the masochist* with equal satisfaction in a sadomasochistic scenario*   "Can switch, but prefer dominant" (personal ad, adult bookstore, Columbus, Ohio, 2/27/87). **2:**   *v* (*OED* 1611, 'strike with a switch')   *See* whip   (2).   **3:**   *n*   (*OED*   1592,   'slender   riding whip')   *See* whip (1)   "She circled me for several minutes continuing to make the switch whistle through the air" (*SM Express* no. 24: 11, col. 1). *Also* whipcord, whip stick.   **-able   1:**   *n* (probably 20th century)   Sadomasochist who can play the role of either the sadist or the masochist with equal satisfaction   "I'm a male switchable who's into panty fantasies" (personal ad, adult bookstore, Columbus,   Ohio,   2/26/87).   *Also*   dual,   middle. **2:**   *adj*   (probably 20th century)   Able to play the role of either the sadist or the masochist with equal satisfaction   "Bi switchable, very flexible, wishes to meet other males, females, couples, for B & D" (personal ad, restroom wall, bar, Columbus, Ohio, 3/11/87). *Also* dual, middle.

switching keys   *v phr* (probably 20th century)   Advertise one's availability for the opposite role from what one is accustomed to in a sadomasochistic relationship   "You might say that so-and-so is 'switching keys' if they've been a dom all their life and suddenly they advertise as a slave, something like that" (personal interview, "Lucinda," 2/19/87). Keys, like variously colored handkerchiefs, can be worn in S and M bars to advertise one's availability as either a slave* (if worn on the left side) or a master* (if worn on the right).

tape   1:   *n*   (*OED* c. 1000)   Device used to inflict pain on the body of the masochist,* which device typically has all the characteristics of standard masking tape with the exception that its "down side" is extra sticky, so that when it is removed from the human skin it frequently entails removal of the skin as well. **2:** *v* (*OED* 1609) Apply tape to a masochist as described in sense 1 (*CBD*, p. 1, ad for tape).

taskmaster *n* (*OED* 1530, 'one who imposes work, especially heavy work'; probably 20th century) Sadist* "TASKMASTER: The taskmaster trains his slave girl by the [*sic*] means of spanking and paddling" (*Women in Command* no. 16: 9). *Also* corporalist, dom, dominant, left hip pocket, M (3), master, S, (2), sender, sir, top.

tea *n* (Spears early 18th century, 'urine'; probably 20th century) Feces, as that during a Boston tea party* "You suck my cock and I'll lick your ass and eat your tea" (personal ad, adult bookstore, Columbus, Ohio, 4/5/87).

teach *v* (*OED* c. 900, 'show, instruct'; probably 20th century) Instruct through discipline in a sadomasochistic scenario*; the instruction may be to a novice,* but just as often the "teacher/student" relationship is merely role playing on the parts of the participants in the scenario "I teach singles, couples, TVs, bis" (personal ad, adult bookstore, Columbus, Ohio, 3/30/87) **-er** *n* (*OED* 14th century, 'one who shows, instructs') One who teaches in the manner described in sense 1 "Young attractive slave needs teacher to dominate me" (personal ad, restroom wall, bar, Columbus, Ohio, 1/29/87). *Also* tutor (*n*, *v*).

tease *v* (*OED* 1627, 'annoy or vex with persistent action'; *OED* 1812, 'flog'; probably 20th century) Tantalize; annoy, as through the use of incomplete acts of sadomasochism **-ing** *n* (*OED* 1865, 'flogging'; probably 20th century) Annoyance, as described in sense 1 "I'm into bondage, discipline, all cultures, teasing, whatever you like" (personal ad, adult bookstore, Columbus, Ohio, 2/28/87).

Also teasing/denial.   **-er**   (probably 20th century) One who teases as described in sense 1   "I'm no teaser, I'm into heavy B & D" (personal ad, adult bookstore, Columbus, Ohio, 4/14/87).

teasing/denial   *n phr* (see etym. note at teasing; probably 20th century)   *See* teasing. See citation at equestrian.

tele-dom   *n* (probably 20th century)   Dominatrix* who does all or most of her intimidation, domination, and abuse over the telephone   "TELE-DOM: be dominanted [*sic*] by telephone. $35. to MC/VISA" (*Women in Command* no. 16: 25).

tickle   *v* (*OED* 1801, 'lightly tease an area of the skin'; probably 20th century)   In a sadomasochistic scenario,* lightly tease the skin of the submissive,* frequently to the point of pain   **-ing**   *n*   (*OED* 1398, 'act of lightly teasing the skin'; probably 20th century)   Act of lightly teasing the skin in a sadomasochistic scenario, as described in sense 1   "All fantasies and fetishes performed, tickling my specialty" (personal ad, adult bookstore, Columbus, Ohio, 4/2/87).

tidy pain   *n phr* (see etym. note at pain; probably 20th century)   Pain* in a sadomasochistic scenario* that is within the preset limits of the submissive* and which gives erotic pleasure   "Into all cultures, tidy pain only" (personal ad, adult bookstore, Columbus, Ohio, 2/18/87).

time buying   *n phr* (probably 20th century)   Slave exchange,* usually limited to a specified period of time, such as a weekend (*Women in Command* no. 16: 8, questionnaire). *See also* trading.

time waster   *n phr* (probably 20th century)   Sadomasochist who practices only light* sadomasochism   "No time wasters or weaklings" (*Club*, March 1977, p. 22, Karl Steiner glossary).

tit bondage   *n phr* (probably 20th century)   *See* breast torture   "Sometimes tit bondage can result in a woman losing her nipples, something like that, but mostly it just causes bruises—it's pretty harmless stuff" (personal interview, Briar Rose, S/M Women's Support Group, Columbus, Ohio, 2/27/87). *Also* nipple bondage, nipple breast bondage, nipple discipline, nipple restraint, nipple torture, nt, tit discipline, tit torture, titty bondage, titty discipline, titty torture, tt.

tit discipline   *n phr, v phr* (probably 20th century) *See* breast torture   "I'm the best in the business when it comes to tit discipline, spanking, all forms of abuse" (personal interview, "Lady in Black," 3/18/87). *Also* nipple bondage, nipple breast bondage, nipple discipline, nipple restraint, nipple torture, nt, tit discipline, tit torture, titty bondage, titty discipline, titty torture, tt.

tit fucking   *n phr* (probably 20th century)   Masturbation by the male between the breasts of the female   "Desperate for tit fucking" (*Intimate* 1, no. 1: 14, personal ad). *See also* fuck tits.

tit torture   *n phr, v phr* (probably 20th century)   *See* breast torture   "Young slave, requires bare ass spankings and tit torture" (*Bizarre Lifestyles* 1, no. 1: 54, personal ad). *Also* nipple bondage, nipple breast bondage, nipple discipline, nipple restraint, nipple torture, nt, tit bondage, tit discipline, titty bondage, titty discipline, titty torture, tt.

titty bondage   *n phr* (probably 20th century)   *See* breast torture   "Titty bondage is the best turnon" (graffito, restroom wall, bar, Columbus, Ohio, 1/28/87). *Also* nipple bondage, nipple breast bondage, nipple discipline, nipple restraint, nipple torture, nt, tit bondage, tit discipline, tit torture, titty discipline, titty torture, tt.

titty bottle   *n phr* (probably 20th century)   Baby bottle, especially one used in infantilism.* See citation at infantalism.

titty discipline   *n phr, v* (probably 20th century)   *See* breast torture   As in "You've never experienced real titty discipline until you've felt my chains around your body!" (information supplied by the vice squad, Columbus Police Dept., 3/7/87). *Also* nipple bondage, nipple breast bondage, nipple discipline, nipple restraint, nipple torture, nt, tit bondage, tit discipline, tit torture, titty bondage, titty torture, tt.

titty torture   *n phr, v* (probably 20th century)   *See* breast torture   "I'll whip your ass and bind your tits—titty torture is my specialty, and you must call me today!" (personal ad, restroom wall, bar, Columbus, Ohio, 12/10/86). *Also* nipple bondage, nipple breast bondage, nipple discipline, nipple restraint, nipple torture, nt, tit bondage, tit discipline, tit torture, titty bondage, titty discipline, tt.

titty twister   *n   phr* (probably 20th century)
1:   Device used in sadomasochistic relationships to inflict pain on the breasts and especially the nipples of the masochist*; titty twisters come in a variety of styles, but all have in common the characteristic of having nipple clamps* that can be made to rotate once in position, thus twisting the breasts or nipples of the person wearing the device.
2:   Movement associated with the use of the device described in sense 1 (*CBD*, p. 5, ad for titty twisters).

tit-whip   *v* (probably 20th century)   Kind of breast torture* involving flagellation of the submissive's* breasts, usually with a small cat-o-nine-tails   **-ing**   *n*   (probably 20th century)   Action of torturing a submissive's breasts as described in sense 1   "Overwhelmed by these Big Busted Babes, he is smothered, tit whipped and teased" (*Women in Command* no. 16: 12, videotape ad).

toilet   *n* (*OED* 1819, 'bathroom'; probably 20th century)   *See* toilet slave   "I will be your toilet, your complete slave" (personal ad, adult bookstore, Columbus, Ohio, 4/23/87).

toilet service   *n phr* (see etym. note at toilet; probably 20th century)   *See* toilet training (*Women in Command* no. 16: 8, questionnaire). *Also toilet servitude, toilet sex.*

toilet servitude   *n phr* (see etym. note at toilet; probably 20th century)   *See* toilet training   "Slave with ample experience in toilet servitude needs new guidance from domineering master" (personal ad, adult bookstore, Columbus, Ohio, 2/22/87). *Also* toilet service, toilet sex.

toilet sex   *n phr* (see etym. note at toilet; probably 20th century)   *See* toilet training   "Dominant has need for clean toilet sex" (personal ad, adult bookstore, Columbus, Ohio, 3/11/87). *Also* toilet service, toilet servitude.

toilet slave   *n phr* (see etym. notes at slave, toilet)   Submissive* who receives golden showers* and brown showers,* perhaps to the extent of ingesting the urine and/or feces   "Unhurried, she squatted down and positioned herself over my mouth. 'Open,' she ordered. 'Don't worry, I'm so healthy that my piss will be good for you.' And she began to piss in my mouth. When she sensed that my mouth was full, she would briefly stop so that I could swallow. 'Enjoy it, I love pissing in my slaves' faces, in their hair and in their mouths, so you'd better get used to it. My female slave is already an accomplished toilet slave.' When she finished, she ordered me to dry her with my tongue" (*Corporal* 10. no. 3: 5–6). *Also* toilet. *See also* urinal.

toilet train   *v* (see etym. note at toilet; probably 20th century)   Give and receive golden showers* and brown showers* in a sadomasochistic relationship   **-ing**   *n* (probably 20th century)   Giving and receiving of golden showers and brown showers in a sadomasochistic relationship   "I need a stern master that can put and keep me in with discipline, humiliation, toilet training, etc." (*Bizarre Lifestyles* 1, no. 1: 48, personal ad). *Also* toilet service, toilet servitude, toilet sex.

token   *n* (*OED* 1655, 'evidence'; probably 20th century) *See* token of sincerity   "Small token appreciated" (personal ad, adult bookstore, Columbus, Ohio, 3/12/87).

token of sincerity   *n phr* (see etym. note at token; probably 20th century)   Money, as that given for professional sadomasochistic services performed   "I cater best to those who offer tokens of sincerity" (personal ad, adult bookstore, Columbus, Ohio, 4/1/87). *Also* token. *See also* generous, sincere.

top   *n* (*OED* 1627, 'chief position'; probably 20th century)   *See* sadist   As in "Top has lost bottom, seeks new same" (see Samois 1982, 31). *Also* corporalist, dom, dominant, left hip pocket, M (3), master, S (2), sender, sir, taskmaster.

torture   **1:**   *n* (*OED* 1551, 'deliberate infliction of pain on one by another, especially that done for the enjoyment of the person inflicting it'; probably 20th century)   In a sadomasochistic scenario,* the infliction of pain or torment on the masochist* by the sadist.* **2:**   *v*   (*OED* 1593, 'deliberately inflict pain on another, especially for the enjoyment derived from inflicting it'; probably 20th century)   Inflict pain in a sadomasochistic scenario as described in sense 1   "This dom knows no bounds, can torture you beyond all known limits of pleasure" (personal ad, adult bookstore, Columbus, Ohio, 1/12/87). The difference between *torture* in the conventional meaning of the word and sadomasochistic *torture* is that the former knows no bounds except those imposed by the torturer, whereas the latter has very definite bounds set by the one being tortured.

total   *adj* (*OED* 1647, 'complete')   Complete and merciless, within the bounds of the sadomasochistic scenario*   "I'm into total domination" (personal ad, adult bookstore, Columbus, Ohio, 3/30/87). Often used in combination, as in total petticoat discipline.*

total petticoat domination   *n phr* (see etym. notes at total and petticoat discipline; probably 20th century)   Petticoat discipline* that is total*   "B and D couple, mid 40s, into fetishes, total petticoat discipline, showers of all kinds" (personal ad, adult bookstore, Columbus, Ohio, 3/2/87).

toys   *n   pl* (*OED* 1586, 'plaything'; probably 20th century)   Implements used in bondage and discipline* and sadomasochistic activities   "Most complete line of toys available anywhere—we have EVERYTHING you need to bring you and your partners to new heighths [*sic*] of pain and pleasure" (ad, adult bookstore, Columbus, Ohio, 3/12/87). *Also* equipment.

trade   *v* (*OED* 1628, 'exchange goods'; probably 20th century)   Exchange one submissive* for another between dominants*   **trading**   *n* (*OED* 1590, 'exchange of goods'; probably 20th century)   *See* slave exchange (*Women in Command* no. 16: 8, questionnaire). *Also* time buying.

train   *v* (*OED* 1542, 'instruct and discipline'; probably 20th century)   Teach a submissive* to be a slave* to the dominant*; inflict any kind of discipline,* humiliation,* or bondage* on another. *Also* sextrain   **training**   *n* (*OED* 1548, 'instruction and discipline in some occupation'; probably 20th century)   Teaching of a submissive as described in sense 1   "Will train beginning slaves in total servitude" (*Intimate* 1, no. 1: 49, personal ad). *Also* obedience training, sextraining. Train(ing) is often used in combination, as in training room, toilet train(ing), TV training, etc.

training room   *n phr* (see etym. note at training; probably 20th century)   Dungeon*   "Fully equipped training room" (*Women in Command* no. 16: 25, personal ad). *Also* mardi gras room, playroom.

trample   *v* (*OED* 1382, 'tread heavily, stamp'; probably 20th century)   Step on a submissive,* usually with spiked

heels, as a means of discipline* and humilia-
tion*   **trampling**   n (OED c. 1440, 'act of treading heavily'; probably 20th century)   Stepping on a submissive as
described in sense 1   "Foot, shoe and boot fetishism,
trampling and toilet slavery my specialties" (Corporal 10, no.
3: 38 personal ad). Also high heel discipline, high heel training, spike action.

transvestite   n (W9 c. 1922)   Male who dresses and
acts like a woman, especially privately, for purposes of emotional and/or sexual gratification   "I specialize in transvestites" (Bizarre Lifestyles 1, no. 1: 41, personal ad). Also
TV, T.V. See also crossdress (-ing).

travel   v (OED 1290, 'journey'; probably 20th century) Go
relatively long distance to consummate a sadomasochistic
relationship, often for pay; travel frequently entails inter-
state journeys   "Can travel nationally" (Bizarre Lifestyles
1, no. 1: 43, personal ad).

true   adj   (OED 1398, 'real, genuine'; probably 20th
century)   See real   Used only in combination, as in true
masochism,* true sadism,* etc.

true masochism   n phr (see etym. notes at true and masochism; probably 20th century)   See real masochism   "A lot of people think they're into masochism, but
they're really not. True masochism is pretty heavy stuff" (personal interview, "Lady in Black," 3/18/87)   **-ist**   n
phr   (see etym. notes at true and masochist; probably 20th
century)   See real masochist   "True masochist has
never found anybody who can dominate him" (personal ad,
adult bookstore, Columbus, Ohio, 3/23/87).

true sadism   n phr (see etym. notes at true and sadism;
probably 20th century)   See real sadism   "Ditto true
sadism" (personal interview,"Lady in Black," 3/18/87)
-ist   n phr (see etym. notes at true and sadist; probably
20th century)   See real sadist   "If you have been look-

ing for a true sadist who can master you totally, call or write"
(personal ad, adult bookstore, Columbus, Ohio, 2/22/87).

truth or dare *n phr* (probably 20th century)   Sadomasochistic game for two or more players
based on the drinking game of the same name; in the game,
a player chooses either to tell the truth about a matter or to
take some specified dare, and if he or she does not tell the
truth or complete the dare to the satisfaction of the other
players, must endure some kind of sadomasoch-
ism   "Experienced truth or dare players needed, no heavy
pain" (personal ad, restroom wall, OSU main library, 4/4/87).

TS   *n* (probably 20th century)   Transsexual; one who
has been surgically transformed from a member of one gender into a member of the other   "Attractive submissive
educated Bi-male will slave for dominants, women, couples,
guys, TS's" (*Intimate* 1, no. 1: 26, personal ad).

tt   *n phr, v* (probably 20th century)   *See* breast torture.
See citation at nt. *tt* is an abbreviation of tit(ty) torture.* *Also*
nipple bondage, nipple breast bondage, nipple discipline,
nipple restraint, nipple torture, nt, tit bondage, tit discipline,
tit torture, titty bondage, titty discipline, titty torture.

tutor   *n, v* (*OED* 1861, *n*, 'master charged with supervi-
sion of a particular boy'; probably 20th century; *OED* 1592,
v, 'instruct with discipline')   *See* teacher   "Greek and
French tutor wanted" (personal ad, adult bookstore, Columbus, Ohio, 3/31/87).

TV   *n* (probably 20th century)   *See* transvestite   "My slave stable has a few vacancies and must be filled
immediately with TV's and docile males" (*Bizarre Lifestyles*
1, no. 1: 52, personal ad). *Also* T.V.

TV discipline   *n phr* (see etym. notes at TV and discipline;
probably 20th century)   *See* TV training   "My imagination and expertise in humiliation, slave training, spanking

TV discipline [*sic*] are unsurpassed" (*Bizarre Lifestyles* 1, no. 1: 55, personal ad).

TV training   *n phr* (see etym. notes at TV and training; probably 20th century)   Discipline* and humiliation* of a transvestite   "I specialize in all kinds of domination: verbal abuse, golden shower, brown shower, TV training, foot worship, castration, B/D, S/M, spanking & enema" (*Bizarre Lifestyles* no. 84: 31, personal ad). *Also* TV discipline.

T.V.   *n* (probably 20th century)   *See* TV   "Sexy full-bodied Mistress seeks submissive males, females, T.V.'s to serve her along with current T.V. slave" (*B & D Pleasures* no. 56: 20, personal ad). *Also* transvestite.

U/C   *adj* (probably 20th century)   Uncut; uncircumcised   "Male, 22, 5'10", 147 lbs., 7", U/C, seeks pleasurable encounters with TVs" (personal ad, adult bookstore, Columbus, Ohio, 3/4/87). Uncut males are of special interest to dominants* because special clamps can be applied to the foreskin.

understanding   *adj* (probably 20th century)   Willing to respect personal limits*   "Skilled 26 yr. old white mistress seeks submissive males, TV's, couples, (Females welcome) for strict yet understanding discipline" (*Bizarre Lifestyles* 1, no. 1: 46 personal ad).

urinal   *n* (*OED* 1851, 'enclosure for the receiving of urine'; probably 20th century)   Submissive* who especially enjoys being urinated on   "Let me be your urinal; also into panty gags, etc. (personal ad, adult bookstore, Columbus, Ohio, 2/12/87). *See also* toilet slave.

vacation   **1:**   *n* (probably 20th century)   One-night stand; sadomasochistic relationship that lasts for only one scenario.*   **2:**   *v*   (probably   20th   century)

Participate in a one-night stand; participate in a sadomasochistic relationship that lasts for only one scenario "Young woman, well endowed, fulfills all fantasies, vacations only" (personal ad, adult bookstore, Columbus, Ohio, 2/22/87). Vacations are especially popular among people who pay or receive pay for engaging in sadomasochistic relationships. **-er** *n* (probably 20th century) Person who vacations, as explained in sense 2 "Vacationer looking for light S/M" (personal ad, adult bookstore, Columbus, Ohio, 2/12/87). Frequently occurs in the phrase *vacationers welcome*.

vanilla sex *n phr* (probably 20th century) Conventional sexual intercourse "Into everything, bored with vanilla sex" (personal ad, adult bookstore, Columbus, Ohio, 3/1/87).

velvet *n* (probably 20th century) Sadomasochism or sadomasochistic activities of any kind (*Blue Velvet* [popular movie of 1987]). *Velvet* is a code word signalling that the user is interested in sadomasochism in some way, shape, or form, and is frequently used in combination, as in velvet rope.*

velvet rope *n phr* (probably 20th century) *See* crotch rope. (*CBD*, p. 2, ad for velvet rope).

velvet underground *n phr* (probably 20th century) Subculture of sadomasochism* "Novice seeks intro. to velvet underground" (personal ad, restroom wall, OSU main library, 3/12/87).

versatile *adj* (*OED* 1656, 'characterized by readiness or facility in turning from one pursuit or task to another'; probably 20th century) Pertaining to a person who has a wide range of sadomasochistic interests and who can serve with equal gratification as either the dominant* or the submissive* "I like it all, am extremely versatile" (personal ad, adult bookstore, Columbus, Ohio, 2/19/87).

vertical bra   *n phr* (see etym. note at horizontal bra; probably 20th century)   Kind of device used in sadomasochistic relationships to inflict pain on the breasts of the female masochist*; vertical bras are constructed similarly to standard brassieres with the exception that they are typically made of leather or metal and allow the breasts to be pulled in opposite directions on the vertical plane (*B & D Pleasures* no. 56: 29, ad for vertical bras). *See also* horizontal bra.

wand   *n* (*OED* c. 1200, 'straight, slender stick'; probably 20th century)   Electrical toy* consisting of a charged stick that can be touched to the body or inserted into various orifices; the wand gives a shock of varying severity to the part of the body with which it comes into contact (*CBD*, p. 11, ad for wands).

warm bottom   *n phr* (probably 20th century)   Buttocks that are flagellated frequently or that have been recently flagellated   "My warm bottom aches to feel the cold slap of your hand" (personal ad, adult bookstore, Columbus, Ohio, 1/28/87).

water lover   *n phr* (probably 20th century)   Dominant* or submissive* who especially enjoys watersports*   "TV's and water lovers welcome" (*Corporal* 10, no. 3: 34, personal ad).

watersports   *n pl* (probably 20th century)   Golden showers* and/or enemas*   "Attractive male, interested in learning more about and exploring bondage, watersports, TV and being a slave to the right woman" (*Bizarre Lifestyles* 1, no. 1: 41, personal ad). *Also* wet sex, WS, W/S, W.S.

wax   *n, v* (probably 20th century)   *See* candle wax torture   "I'm into everything—showers of all kinds, wax, bondage and discipline, heavy pain" (personal ad, restroom wall, OSU main library, 2/26/87). *Also* hot wax, wax torture.

wax torture   *n phr, v* (probably 20th century)   *See* candle wax torture   As in "Let me subdue and torture you— well-stocked dungeon, experienced in exotic practices including wax torture" (information provided by vice squad, Columbus Police Dept., 3/11/87). *Also* hot wax, wax.

wayout   *n, adj* (probably 20th century)   *See* weirdo   "Looking for sane, common-sense partner for B/ D, some S/M. No wayouts, please" (personal ad, restroom wall, bar, Columbus, Ohio, 2/11/87).

weakling   *n* (*OED* 1526, 'effeminate person'; probably 20th century)   Man with an exceptionally small penis. See citation at time waster.

weekend scenario   *n phr* (probably 20th century)   Scenario* that may extend over an entire weekend   "Seek submissive and dom/sub couples to safely share moments in exhibitionism, humiliation, B&D, teasing, body worship, evening/weekend scenarios" (*B & D Pleasures* no. 56: 28, personal ad).

weekend service   *n phr* (probably 20th century)   Sadomasochistic relationships occurring on weekends; *weekend service* is frequently used by a professional dominatrix* to let potential customers know that she works Saturdays and Sundays (*Women in Command* no. 16: 8, questionnaire).

weird   *adj* (*OED* 1820, 'out of the ordinary')   Pertaining to a fetish, practice, or behavior that is, in the mind of the user of the word, extreme or dangerous, or a person desiring such behavior   **—o**   *n* (*W9* 1959, 'one exhibiting extraordinarily strange behavior'; probably 20th century)   One who has a fetish, practice, or behavior as described in sense 1   "Dominant bi, 32, seeks partner for watersports, including piss enemas. No weirdos, please" (personal ad, adult bookstore, Columbus, Ohio, 3/11/87). *Also* way out. *See also* kink.

wet sex   n phr (probably 20th century)   See watersports   "TV into water sports would like to swing" (personal
ad, adult bookstore, Columbus, Ohio, 1/26/87). Also WS,
W/S, W.S.

whip   **1:**   n (OED 1325, 'instrument for flagellation')   Instrument, usually made of leather, metal, or hard
wood, used for whipping or lashing masochists.* Also switch
(n), whipcord, whip stick. **2:**   v (OED 1386, 'strike with a
whip)   Flagellate as explained in sense 1. Also switch
(v)   **-ing**   n   (OED   1366,   'action   of   flagellation')   Flagellation as explained in sense 1   "Experience
real S/M, bondage, erotic torture, humiliation games, whippings" (Corporal 10, no. 3: 38, personal ad).

whipcord   n (OED 1318–19, 'thin, tough hempen cord
used for whipping')   See whip (1)   "I'm afraid there is
nothing else for you, sweety. It's time you felt some whipcord"
(SM Express no. 24: 9). Also switch (n), whipstick.

whip off   v (probably 20th century)   Experience an orgasm while whipping or being whipped during a sadomasochistic scenario*   "Come tan my pretty fanny so I can
whip off" (personal ad, adult bookstore, Columbus, Ohio, 2/
12/87).

whip stick   n (probably 20th century)   See whip
(1)   "When you resume the whipping the lashes of the
whip stick on [sic] the body for a tiny moment longer" (SM
Express no. 24: 8, cols. 2–3). Also switch (n), whipcord.

white sugar   n phr (probably 20th century)   White
(usually female) sadomasochist   "Looking for a little white
sugar to experience REAL domination at the hands of a black
MAN" (personal ad, restroom wall, bar, Columbus, Ohio,2/
27/87). See also brown sugar.

women's libber   n   phr   (probably   20th   century)   Sadistic lesbian or bisexual   "White, 23, 32–22–

34, seeks women's libber for mutual satisfaction; into masturbation, greek, light bondage" (personal ad, adult bookstore, Columbus, Ohio, 1/16/87). Rare.

work for major airline   *v phr* (probably 20th century)   Can travel*   "Bi-female, 23, work for major airline, practice most fetishes and fantasies" (personal ad, adult bookstore, Columbus, Ohio, 3/23/87).

worship   1:   *n*   (*OED* c. 888, 'highest esteem')   Complete devotion in a sadomasochistic scenario*   "I want your full worship" (personal ad, adult bookstore, Columbus, Ohio, 2/19/87). **2:**   *v* (*OED* c. 1200 'honor, revere as supernatural being')   Show complete   devotion   to   in   a   sadomasochistic   scenario   "WARNING: If you call, I will make you worship me" (personal ad, adult bookstore, Columbus, Ohio, 1/30/87). See notes to body worship.

WS   *n phr* (probably 20th century)   *See* watersports   "Must be into WS or don't bother to write" (personal ad, adult bookstore, Columbus, Ohio, 2/11/87). *Also* wet sex, W/S, W.S.

W/S   *n phr* (probably 20th century)   *See* watersports   "Male, 31, seeks attractive women for all forms of erotic sexuality; B&D, W/S, cane and roll [*sic*] playing" (*Bizarre Lifestyles* 1, no. 1: 43, personal ad). *Also* wet sex, W.S

W.S.   *n phr* (probably 20th century)   *See* watersports   "Are you there, dominant? I ache for W.S., bondage, the works!" (personal ad, restroom wall, OSU main library, 3/9/87). *Also* wet sex, W/S.

yellow   *inter* (probably 20th century)   Safe word* used when the submissive* wants the dominant* to slow the intensity of the scenario* (see Weinberg 1983, 379). *See also* green, red (1).

yellow handkerchief   *n   phr*   (probably 20th century)   Sadomasochist who especially enjoys watersports*   As in "I've lost a brand new yellow handkerchief and now need to locate another new or used one" (information provided by vice squad, Columbus Police Dept., 3/11/87). In an S & M bar, a person wearing a yellow handkerchief is advertising that he or she is looking for a person with whom to enjoy watersports.

Form and Substance in the Language of Sadomasochism

Thus far we have represented the language of sadomasochism as merely a glossary of approximately 800 words and phrases. In this section, however, we would like to take a more substantive approach to that terminology: What notable patterns, if any, does this specialized language contain? How can it best be characterized, both by comparison to the English language as a whole and as an entity unto itself? And how does the language seem to reflect the concerns and preoccupations of the people who use it?

On first looking at the glossary, one may be struck by the high proportion of terms that are nominals—nearly 80 percent—as compared to the relative paucity of verbals—about 15 percent—and adjectivals—only about 5 percent. But these figures closely parallel most experts' best guesses for the English language as a whole: while a precise count cannot be made because of constant additions to, deletions from, and function shifts within the language, it is an accepted fact that English has always been and continues to be an overwhelmingly nominalizing language. In fact, in a study of new words entering the language between 1963 and 1973, John Algeo discovered proportions of new nouns and verbs almost identical to those given above, concluding that in English "there are far more new things than new events to talk about" (1980, 272).

Of greater interest, perhaps, is the high incidence of initialisms in the language of sadomasochism: nearly 10 percent of the terms collected are single letters (e.g., *A*, *B*, *E*, *F*, *G*), combinations of letters (*BD*, *BS*, *SM*), or letters used in conjunction with full words (*C & B torture*). Indeed, some personal ads seem to be nothing but an endless string of initialisms:

SWM seeks SOF for BD, SM, GS and BS, E, F, G, etc.
[From an adult bookstore, Columbus, Ohio, 4/15/87]

This tendency to abbreviate no doubt reflects the influence of personal ads on the shaping of the language: because such ads are the most popular method of communication between would-be partners, and because such ads become more expensive as the number of words (or, occasionally, the number of lines) increases, of course *BD* is cheaper to write than *bondage and discipline*. Moreover, daily newspapers usually prohibit personal ads that solicit sex in any form, and coded initialisms are one way of obviating the problem of how to communicate, for example, *golden shower* and *brown shower*.

Also of interest is what might be called the "character" of the terms comprising the language of sadomasochism. We should not be surprised, perhaps, to discover that among the many metaphorical patterns to be found there are **fantasy** (*golden shower, golden nuggets, geisha slave, golden nectar, maid service, on the moon, role play, toy*), **violence and pain** (*anal rape, cock and ball torture, catfighting, birching, beat the brains out, whipping*), and **discipline** (*corporal discipline, corporal punishment, correction, discipliness, dun-*

geon, headmistress, masturbation punishment, paddle, total petticoat discipline). These concepts lie at the very heart of sadomasochism, and are rightly well represented in its language. Equally well represented, however, are the metaphorical patterns of **sophistication** (*arts, backgammon, educated, cultures, goddess, social*) and **neutrality** (*basket, back yard, bib, blanket, bracelet, pony, tape, blue handkerchief*)—both perhaps products of the highly euphemistic nature of the language and, again, the need to publish personal ads in publications that would frown on the use of anything other than this kind of heavily coded language.

Though mentioned briefly above, it is perhaps worth making the point again that the language of sadomasochism is highly euphemistic. As is the case with most other underworld jargons, it seems to be attempting to conceal the socially unacceptable activities and practices of those who use it. Consider, for example, terms such as *back parlor, beefsteak and onions, watersports, wax, vacation*, and *bracelet*. None of these calls to mind anything other than positive images for most people—a favorite room of the house, a tasty sandwich, fun in a swimming pool, a candle burning, an extended pleasure trip, a treasured piece of jewelry; yet each symbolizes for the members of this subculture an entirely different kind of thing or event—the buttocks and anus, unreserved sadomasochism, the giving of enemas and the urinating of one person on another, feces, a one-night sadomasochistic relationship, and a specially made or decorated ornament for the wrist. Or, perhaps better, consider the following two personal ads, the second being a relatively mild "translation" of the first:

Need education in French and Greek; know English well. Afterwards let's share beefsteak and onions. Also enjoy watersports of all kinds. [From an adult bookstore, Columbus, Ohio, 3/26/87]

I need someone to introduce me to oral and anal sex; I'm already experienced in the whipping and flogging of buttocks. Afterwards, let's share some no-holds-barred sadomasochism. I also enjoy giving and receiving enemas as well as urinating on others and having them urinate on me.

Granted, the two ads convey very different overall messages—the second seems at once both too literate and too crude, and probably would not elicit many responses—but on some level they "say" the same thing. Perhaps the biggest difference between the two is that whereas the first could occur in any personals column, the second could not.

But if the language of sadomasochism is euphemistic, it is not entirely so; indeed, it can, at times, be equally straightforward: terms such as *ass plug, ball stretcher, bondage, breast press, cockblock, forced enema, fistfuck, nipple clamp*, and a host of others leave very little to the imagination and certainly make no attempt to lessen the connotative or denotative impact of the language. Quite the contrary: they seem to exist almost in defiance of mainstream English and the taboo-filled culture with which it is so closely associated, at once both reviling and enticing those people who use them. Consider the following rather lengthy personal ad:

If you've been fantasizing about a hot pussy, I'm your girl. I'm 5'9", 126 lbs., 38D-23-36, and can't wait to wrap my lips around your prick and give you the blowjob of your life. You can spank my bottom and soothe it down by showering it with love and kisses, then eat me till I'm dry. Got a fantasy? I can help make it come true. [From an adult bookstore, Columbus, Ohio, 2/15/87]

To say that this ad is frank would be understating the facts, but that frankness only ads to its sensuous, alluring quality. Had more conventional language been used, the ad would have taken on much more the quality of clinical sterility:

If you need a sexual companion, I'm your girl. I'm tall, slender, and well-built, and will fellate you. I'm also agreeable to English if you'll soothe me and perform

cunnilingus on me. Got a fantasy? I can help make
it happen.

Most personal ads seems to be a blend of the straightforward
and the euphemistic, as though the writer were trying to
achieve some delicate balance of propriety and temptation.
And the language of sadomasochism—precisely because it
allows a range of style-shifts from the blatant to the under-
stated—is especialy well suited for the task of achieving this
balance.

Perhaps because so much of the language of sadomasochism must be contrived by individuals who seek to impart
to their personal ads something inventive and out of the
ordinary (and perhaps also because identical original coinages by two people seeking to describe the same act are exceedingly rare), we find that language filled with clusters of
synonyms. *Breast torture*, for example, is also known as *nipple bondage, nipple breast bondage, nipple discipline, nipple torture, tit bondage, titty bondage, tit discipline, titty
discipline, tit torture, titty torture*, and *tt*; and *penis punishment* can also be referred to as *pp, penis bondage, penis
torture, pp*, and *pt*. Clearly, lexicographic frugality is not the
rule here, and especially so with the most frequently used
and abused body parts as well as the most frequent practices.
Similarly, not many of the terms reported in the glossary
have more than one referent; in fact, fewer than 5 percent
do. This again points to the influence of the "personal ads"
method of communication, for surely misunderstandings
cannot be afforded in such a permanent (i.e., written and
hence unchangeable until the next ad appears) and often
highly telegraphic medium.

One might properly wonder if the language of sadomasochism did not share a good many terms with the other
underworld subcultures with which it has something significant in common, prostitution and homosexuality. The
answer, predictably, is that sadomasochism and each of
these other two subcultures share only those terms reflecting
the points of subcultural overlap. Many prostitutes, for example, prefer servicing their clients orally rather than vagi-

nally (because, putatively, such servicing leaves their makeup intact, thus saving them valuable time between customers); thus *French* is a common term among users of that argot. Similarly, oral sexual gratification plays a large part in homosexuality and sadomasochism as well, and *French* is also well known among members of those subcultures. *Greek*, on the other hand, is much more a part of sadomasochism and homosexuality than prostitution (anal penetration consumes more time and is more dangerous to the prostitute than the more conventional methods of sexual release), so it is much more a part of the sadomasochist's and homosexual's lexicons than the prostitute's. Consider also that in recent years some professional dominatrices have again turned to selling their talents ("again" because sadomasochistic birchings and floggings seem to have been fairly common in Victorian brothels); thus several terms common to the lingo of "straight" prostitution have made their way into the argot of prostitutional sadomasochism as well—e.g., *sincere*, *generous*, *hustle*, and *token of generosity*. And transvestism and sodomy—both of which occur in sadomasochism and in homosexuality—have lent terms such as *transvestite*, *crossdress*, *back yard*, and *back parlor* to the argots of these subcultures. In short, then, the linguistic and cultural relationships among sadomasochism, prostitution, and homosexuality are complex: sadomasochism has its own specialized language, some of the terms of which it shares in common with homosexuality, some others of which with prostitution, and some of which with both homosexuality and prostitution.

As to the question of which subject areas account for most of the terms in the language of sadomasochism, the answer is again quite predictable. Nearly 50 percent of the terms specify practices, procedures, or techniques used in sadomasochistic encounters—*anilingus*, *Roman*, *cat fighting*, and so forth—in short, what members of the subculture do to and with one another during their encounters. Another 15 percent define the members of the subculture, usually naming a role played or perceived during a sadomasochistic scenario—e.g., *amazon*, *bitch goddess*, *slut*, and the like.

And the last major category of terms, also numbering approximately 15 percent, refers to the equipment that can be used during the scenarios—*whip, ball gag, horizontal breast press,* and *stock,* among many others.

A somewhat closer scrutiny of the language of sadomasochism yields an unexpected finding: there is a distinct lack of parallelism between nouns and verbs—or, in other words, not always a corresponding verb for a noun (and vice versa), even where such a correspondence could be expected. Because the noun *birching* exists, for example, one might also expect to find the verb *birch*; and because *cage* the noun exists, one can easily imagine *cage* the verb. But we could not find a single occurrence of either *birch* or *cage* the verb, and were similarly frustrated with hundreds of other words. Moreover, we can offer no real explanation for why there should exist such a lack of parallel noun/verb combinations. The possibility does exist, of course, that we simply overlooked them or did not look in the right places for them (but we think this unlikely, given the many places we searched and the thoroughness with which we searched them); or that such parallel structures could well be confined to oral usage, as during a sadomasochistic scenario, as opposed to occurring in personal ads or other written forms of the language (and we did not witness or partake in any scenarios, believing that even the thrill of discovery in research has its limits); or that the parallelisms merely have not surfaced yet, but will at some point in the future (a distinct possibility, considering both that most of the language of sadomasochism is extremely young compared to the subculture itself [see our comments in the paragraph following this one] and that function shifts are extremely common in English); or even that the phenomenon is merely one of the quirks of the language that helps to account for the tendency toward nominalization discussed earlier.

Well over 75 percent of all the terms comprising the language of sadomasochism seem to have originated in the twentieth century (though some of them have semantic roots in earlier centuries, of course). This is an interesting fact, and one made all the more so when we realize that sadomasochism in some form is probably centuries—perhaps millennia—old, and that it was associated with English sexual preferences at least as early as the mid-nineteenth century. Thus the question naturally arises as to why the vernacular of such an extremely old subculture should suddenly begin to multiply, seemingly with no end in sight. Certainly there must have been a perceived need for such an increase, and we believe that this need was engendered, ultimately, by the cultural and social environment in which the users of the language found themselves. Recall that beginning in the 1960s—in conjunction with the liberal attitude with which many Americans approached issues of sexuality—many "sexual deviants" let their deviations from what had heretofore been perceived as the norm be known— they came out of the closet, as it were. Most of the public's attention was focused on homosexuality and bisexuality, but sadomasochism began to surface as well: not only was this the period when personal ads became popular, but the publishing industry began to devote more of its energy and capital to the subculture. This resulted, in short, in members of the subculture who had not known how extensive their membership was suddenly making new contacts and forming new interpersonal networks, the effect of which was increased communication and the need for a highly specialized, often coded language.

From the foregoing remarks, one might suppose that a good many nonce terms were coined in the language of sadomasochism. In fact, a good many were—and were treated in one of two ways, as are all new coinages. Either they died an ignominious death at the hands of Father Time or they eventually became popular enough to be considered a part of the language. In our research, we found very few nonce terms, suggesting that the standard language of sadomasochism is perceived by most of its users as suitable for their needs. Exceptions to this—nonce terms coined perhaps because the individuals using them were being creative—numbered only three, and we present them here in their original contexts:

> **John Norman:** "Creative, intelligent, switchable male, seeking switchable female to exchange training

methods including initiations and John Norman."
(*SM Express* no. 24: 18, personal ad)
P & P: "We're into your scene—even P & P." (*Bizarre Lifestyles* 1, no. 1: 45, personal ad; the "we" of this ad refers to two young women pictured in an accompanying photograph.)
SPEACH Society: [Precise language no longer available; paraphrased, the ad referred to "joining a SPEACH Society,"] (Restroom wall, Main Library, The Ohio State University, February 1987)

We do not know the meaning of these terms. *John Norman* may be a reference to a character in some piece of sadomasochistic literature we have not seen, or may refer to a ritual or practice none of our informants was familiar with; the *p*'s in *P & P* may refer to *pain, pleasure, pets, pals, plastic*, or any number of other terms; and *SPEACH* may be an acronym for a private, not-well-known club. One informant suggested that the writers of these ads included the terms in question simply to spark the curiosity of the readers, thereby ensuring a large response to the ads. We cannot be sure, and the mystery remains unsolved.

Finally, we broach two topics that are among the most interesting to discuss when considering the language of sadomasochism, but that also are among the most difficult to understand for outsiders of the subculture. First, the reader will no doubt have noticed from the glossary that there are many ways of referring to both *bondage and discipline* (or *BD*) and *sadomasochism* (or *SM*), and that the two have very different definitions—that, in short, BD is a specialized form of SM. All of this is correct as far as it goes, but, unfortunately, it does not go far enough. Most members of the sadomasochistic subculture use *BD* and *SM* in connotative ways quite different from their literal meanings—ways that are not captured in the language per se, but exist in the minds of the users nonetheless. BD and SM are most frequently perceived as different *intensities* of sadomasochistic activities rather than different *kinds* of activities, as though *BD* is automatically marked [+ "light"] and *SM* is automatically marked [+ "heavy"]. More interestingly, however, only a very few members of the subculture would ever admit to "being into" SM—even if they regularly engage in scenarios containing legitimate pain and perhaps blood and violence— preferring instead the term *BD*. Linguistically, *BD* is achieving a much broader spectrum of referents, and may eventually become generalized to such an extent that it becomes meaningless; *SM*, on the other hand, is coming to be associated only with the most violent members of the subculture, and hence is undergoing semantic restriction. The members of the subculture are thus losing a valuable means of specifying how intense a scenario they are interested in experiencing, and it will be interesting to see how the language changes to accommodate this loss.

The second interesting topic that demands attention here concerns the medium (Jakobson's "code") of communication in which most of the language of sadomasochism is typically used. In short, the language is by and large a written rather than a spoken entity—a consequence, no doubt, of its primary function of making contact with other as yet unknown members of the subculture. Even in face-to-face encounters—as during initial meetings with prospective partners or during actual scenarios of sadomasochism—the language reported in our glossary often is not used (one notable exception being the previously agreed upon "safe" words); rather, a complex system of body language, including kinesics, proxemics, and haptics, is used in conjunction with a trial-and-error, "feel-your-way" method that most often accomplishes the goals of all interlocutors. There is no good way to catalogue this unspoken paralanguage; suffice it to say that it is a part of the communicative competence that all members of the subculture acquire over time—and that only participation in the subculture will yield more information about it.

This, then, is the form and substance of the language of sadomasochism—a language as versatile and varied as English itself, and one that serves its speakers' needs just as well. This study represents the first full-scale investigation into the language of this subculture, and our intent has been primarily to chronicle its usage. Though we have provided etymological information where possible and have included a brief history of the subculture, our focus remains—out of both desire and necessity—on the synchronic state of the language. We can only hope that others will return to the language of sadomasochism in future generations to begin a diachronic study of how the language has changed since the late 1980s.

Epilogue

In the prefatory comments to our glossary, we made the following observation:

> Though still largely an underground subculture, sadomasochists seem gradually to be coming out of the closet and forming support groups, holding rallies, and even organizing national conventions (lesbian sadomasochists had such a convention in Washington, D.C., in the fall of 1987), all with the intent of fostering greater unity and homogeneity—which homogeneity, we suppose, will naturally extend into their language as well.

Shortly before this book went to press, we learned of a newly formed "National SM/Leather Coalition" that had been created in Dallas, Texas, over the weekend of February 13 and

14, 1988 (which dates, not incidentally, corresponded to Valentine's Day weekend). The coalition, consisting of some 125 people representing over fifty-five sadomasochism-related organizations and businesses from across the United States, followed closely on the heels of the "convention" mentioned briefly above (it was, more accurately, the March on Washington for Lesbian and Gay Rights held on October 11, 1987, and we now know that it had an S/M-Leather contingent that attracted more than 1,000 people to its meetings and workshops). These 125 participants immediately formed an Interim Steering Committee, the first official action of which was to name the coalition Safe-Sane-Consensual Adults (SSCA).

SSCA is pan-sexual (i.e., welcomes all interested parties, without regard to sexual preference or gender), is oriented toward sadomasochism in the broadest sense of the word (i.e., includes S/M, B/D, and all fetishes), and has united all of its members under a working draft of a common "statement of purpose," in which some of the goals of SSCA are stated as follows:

- To help build, strengthen, and defend the S/M, leather, and other fetish communities;

- To promote the rights of adults to engage in all safe, sane, and consensual erotic activities;

- To promote increased communication and cooperation among our organizations, individuals, and businesses around the country;

- To promote education about safe, sane, and consensual behavior within our own communities;

- To convey a more accurate, positive image of our communities;

- To oppose threats to our freedom of expression, our rights to free association, and our rights to equal protection under the law;

- To preserve a record of our history, traditions, and culture.

The statement also includes plans for a national newsletter, a national directory of organizations and businesses, a national calendar of events, a media watch, a speakers' bureau, regular national conferences, and a national archive.

Clearly, our earlier observation is correct—sadomasochists are coming out of the closet—though perhaps more suddenly than gradually. No one can predict what ultimate effect SSCA will have on the sadomasochistic subculture or on the general public's awareness of it, but the reader may recall that in the mid-1950s, a similar group called the Mattachine Society was organized by and for homosexuals. Mattachine made its influence felt almost immediately: more and more homosexuals began identifying themselves openly, organizing marches and rallies, petitioning for legislation aimed at increasing their rights, and, of course, increasing the public's awareness of them and their subculture—including their language.

We decided to write this epilogue because of the axiom that as a subculture grows and changes, so also will the specialized language used by its members grow and change—not just because the language reflects the needs of that subculture, but because, in many ways, it *is* that subculture. The glossary and brief analysis of the language of sadomasochism that we have presented here are valid as of approximately January 1988, but plainly the subculture is beginning to change at an exceedingly fast pace. We therefore reiterate our hope that others will return to the language of sadomasochism in future years so that a complete and accurate chronicle of its dynamic history as well as its then-present state can be maintained.

Notes

INTRODUCTION

1. Unlike the case in most other statistical surveys, researchers report substantial difficulty gathering data that can be considered reliable for a general population, and especially so when dealing with sexual preference (e.g., homosexuality vs. heterosexuality) or preferred methods of sexual activity such as sadomasochism. The most that can realistically be inferred from studies such as Jay and Young's or Spengler's is that they represent the activities and views of those who elect to respond to the questionnaires available to them.

2. As Spengler points out in discussing his method (Weinberg and Kamel 1983, 58), "If one desires to go beyond individual case studies and studies of sadomasochistic prostitution, it is almost impossible to question sadomasochistically oriented women in the subculture; there are hardly any nonprostitutes and very few women in the clubs."

3. For a fuller treatment of the nature of sadomasochism as a subculture and the ways in which the members of that subculture establish the limits of their activity, see Weinberg and Kamel (1983), an excellent collection of articles from a wide variety of sources.

4. The *OED* as well as most standard desk-top dictionaries list *fetich* as a secondary variant of *fetish*. We will use it only when the author/translator does so, and use *fetish* at all other times.

5. The *OED* suggests that keelhauling originated with the Dutch, probably as early as 1560, and shows a first use of the term in English in 1626. Keelhauling is defined as the act of hauling a person "under the keel of a ship, either by lowering him on one side and hauling him across to the other side, or, in the case of smaller vessels, lowering him at the bows and drawing him along under the keel to the stern."

THE LANGUAGE OF SADOMASOCHISM

1. We looked, for example, in journals such as *Alternative Lifestyles, Sexual Medicine Today, Journal of Forensic Medicine, Journal of Abnormal Psychology, Journal of Anthropological Research*, and a host of strictly medical journals too numerous to mention; and in books such as Grahn (1984), Courouve (1985), Ellis (1942), Witting (1979), B. J. Ford (1980), C. S. Ford and Frank (1980), Reik (1941), Randell (1976), Grumley (1977), Goselin and Wilson (1980), Linden et al. (1982), A. Ellis and Abarbane (1967), Martin Goldstein and Haeberle (1971), Jacobs (1974), Brandt (1986), Caplan (1985), Marcus (1981), Carnes (1983), Davis (1983), Lingis (1983), Chasseguel-Smirgel (1984), Stroller (1985), Bryant (1982), Shainess (1984), Zoltano (1971, 1984), Michael Goldstein (1973), Whitehurst (1980), Wolman (1980), Haeberle (1983), and many others.

2. Actually, we did find some interesting lexicographic material, but regarding the language of people who study sadomasochism— that is, their terms for sadomasochists and their practices, such as *algogeñesolagnia, algolagnia*, and *algophily*—rather than those who engage in it.

3. For example, *B & D Pleasures, SM Express, Women in Command, Corporal, Bizarre, Bizarre Lifestyles, Petticoat Power, Wet Letters, B & D Review, Enslave, Bizarre Bitches, Leather Underground*, and a number of others (see Appendix).

4. It would be equally as inaccurate and misleading to report

nonce usages, and we did, of course, find a few. They will be dealt with separately in the discussion following the glossary.

5. There is one inexplicable exception: on the West Coast, *S* is used as an abbreviation for 'slave, submissive', and *M* is used as an abbreviation for 'master'; elsewhere, *S* stands for 'sadist' and *M* stands for 'masochist'. The exception is all the more interesting because of the terms and definitions in question: the terms are so common as to appear in the majority of published ads, and the two definitions for each term are not just different, they are absolute antonyms. No doubt many a non–West Coast person has answered an ad in California (or, conversely, a Californian has answered an ad in another part of the country) only to have his or her expectations completely unfulfilled. Our guess is that this linguistic glitch will follow one of two paths: either the West Coast will eventually adopt the "standard" definitions for *S* and *M* or members of the subculture everywhere will learn and except the West Coast's variation from the "norm." Certainly the present situation of antonymic definitions for the same terms cannot last indefinitely, as it would too often result in a complete breakdown in communication.

References

Algeo, John. 1980. Where Do All the New Words Come From? *American Speech* 55:264–77.

Altman, Dennis. 1982. *The Homosexualization of America*. Boston: Beacon.

Brandt, David. 1986. *Don't Stop Now, You're Killing Me*. New York: Poseidon.

Bryant, Clifton D. 1982. *Sexual Deviancy and Social Proscription: The Social Context of Carnal Behavior*. New York: Human Sciences.

Califia, Pat. 1980. *Saphistry—The Book of Lesbian Sexuality*. Tallahassee: Naiad.

Caplan, P. 1985. *The Myth of Women's Masochism*. New York: E. P. Dutton.

Carnes, P. 1983. *The Sexual Addiction*. Minneapolis: CompCare.

Catalog of Leather Bondage and Restraints. N.d. N.p.

Catalogue of Bondage and Discipline. N.d. N.p.

Chasseguel-Smirgel, Janine. 1984. *Creativity and Perversion*. New York: Norton.

Cleland, John. 1985. *Memoirs of a Woman of Pleasure*. Ed. and intro. by Peter Sabor. Oxford: Oxford University Press.

Courouve, Claude. 1985. *Vocabulaire de l'homosexualité masculine*. Paris: Payot.

Davis, Murray S. 1983. *Smut: Erotic Reality*. Chicago: University of Chicago Press.

Ellis, Albert, and Albert Abarbane. 1967. *The Encyclopedia of Sexual Behavior*. New York: Hawthorn.

Ellis, Havelock. 1942 [1903]. *Studies in the Psychology of Sex*, vol. 2. New York: Random House.

Expose! 1984. New York: Star Distributors.

Ford, Brian John. 1980. *Patterns of Sex: The Mating Urge and Our Sexual Future*. New York: St. Martin's Press.

Ford, Clellan S., and Frank A. Beach. 1980. *Patterns of Sexual Behavior*. Westport, Conn.: Greenwood.

Fuller, Jean Overton. 1968. *Swinburne: A Critical Biography*. London: Chatto and Windus.

Goldstein, Martin and Erwin J. Haeberle. 1971. *The Sex Book: A Modern Encyclopedia*. New York: Herder and Herder.

Goldstein, Michael J. 1973. *A Report of Pornography and Sexual Deviance*. Berkeley: University of California Press.

Goselin, Chris, and Glenn Wilson. 1980. *Sexual Variation*. London: Faber and Faber.

Grahn, Judy. 1984. *Another Mother Tongue: Gay Words, Gay Worlds*. Boston: Beacon.

Greene, Gerald, and Caroline Greene. 1974. *S-M: The Last Taboo*. New York: Grove.

Grumley, Michael. 1977. *Hard Corps: Studies in Leather and Sadomasochism*. New York: E. P. Dutton.

Haeberle, Erwin J. 1983. *The Sex Atlas*. New York: Seabury.

Hawthorne, Nathaniel. 1960. *The Scarlet Letter and Other Tales of the Puritans*. Ed. Harry Levin. Boston: Houghton Mifflin.

Jacobs, Jerry. 1974. *Deviance: Field Studies and Self-disclosures*. Palo Alto, Calif.: National Press Books.

Jay, Karla, and Allen Young. 1979. *The Gay Report: Lesbians and Gay Men Speak Out about Sexual Experiences and Lifestyles*. New York: Summit.

Kinsey, Alfred C., et al. 1948. *Sexual Behavior in the Human Male*. Philadelphia: W. B. Saunders.

———— 1953. *Sexual Behavior in the Human Female*. Philadelphia: W. B. Saunders.

Krafft-Ebing, Richard. 1965 [1885]. *Psychopathia Sexualis*. Trans. Franklin S. Klaf. New York: Bell.

Linden, Robin, et al., eds. 1982. *Against Sadomasochism: A Radical Feminist Analysis*. California: Frog in the Well.

Lingis, Alphonso. 1983. *Excesses: Eros and Culture*. Albany: SUNY Press.

Marcus, Maria. 1981. *A Taste for Pain: On Masochism and Female Sexuality*. Trans. Joan Tate. London: Souvenir.

Poe, Edgar Allen. 1956. *Selected Writings of Edgar Allen Poe*. Ed. Edward H. Davidson. Boston: Houghton Mifflin.

Randell, John. 1976. *Sexual Variations*. Techomic.

Rawson, Hugh. 1981. *A Dictionary of Euphemisms and Other Doubletalk*. New York: Crown.

Reik, Theodor. 1941. *Masochism in Modern Man*. New York: Farrar, Straus and Co.

Samois, ed. 1982. *Coming to Power*. Boston: Alyson.

Schmidt, J. E. 1967. *Lecher's Lexicon*. 2nd ed., 1984. New York: Bell.

Shainess, Natalie. 1984. *Sweet Suffering: Women as Victim*. Indianapolis: Bobbs-Merrill.

Spears, Richard A. 1981. *Slang and Euphemism*. New York: Jonathan David.

Stroller, Robert J. 1985. *Observing the Erotic Imagination*. New Haven, Conn.: Yale University Press.

Weinberg, Thomas, and G. W. Levi Kamel. 1983. *SandM: Studies in Sadomasochism*. Buffalo: Prometheus.

Whitehurst, Robert N. 1980. *The Sexes: Changing Relationships in a Pluralistic Society*. Toronto: Gage.

Witting, Monique. 1979. *Brouillon pour un dictionnaire des amantes/Lesbian Peoples: Material for a Dictionary*. New York: Avon.

Wolman, Benjamin B., ed. 1980. *Handbook of Human Sexuality*. Englewood Cliffs, N.J.: Prentice-Hall.

Zoltano, Rosalie. 1971. *Sexual Latitude, for and Against*. New York: Hart.

———. 1984. *Human Sex Behavior: A Medical Subject Analysis and Research Index*. Washington, D.C.: Abbe.

Appendix: Publications Related to Sexual Sadomasochism

The authors offer this select bibliography to those readers who may have an interest in the study of sexual sadomasochism beyond what can be satisfied by the citations in the References. First we present a list of scholarly and popular sources on sadomasochism, then a list of sadomasochism serials. Though the first group of citations presents sadomasochism from a number of different perspectives (e.g., anthropological, criminal, educational, legal, medical, practical, psychological, sexological, sociological, and so on), it should by no means be interpreted as a comprehensive search of the literature. The second group of citations—also by no means comprehensive—has been annotated where possible; however, because S and M serials as well as their publishers come and go with great frequency (sometimes due to financial problems, but also frequently due to law enforcement agencies or social activist groups), some of the information in the annotations may have changed since this book went to press.

SCHOLARLY AND POPULAR BOOKS AND ARTICLES

Allen, Clifford. 1953. "Some Aspects of Sadism." *International Journal of Sexology* 6: 228–31.

———. 1969. *A Textbook of Psychosexual Disorders*, pp. 47–172. London: Oxford University.

Baggally, W. 1941. "Hedonic Conflict and the Pleasure Principle." *International Journal of Psychoanalysis* 22: 280–300.

Barbara, Dominick A. "Masochism in Love and Sex." *American Journal of Psychoanalysis* 34: 73–79.

Bates, Dorothy. 1975. "Sadomasochists Discuss Their Pleasure . . . and Pain." *Sexology* 42: 11–14, 44.

Berest, Joseph, J. 1970. "Report on a Case of Sadism." *Journal of Sex Research* 6: 210–19.

Beyer, James C., and William F. Enos. 1977. "Obscure Causes of Death During Sexual Activity." *Medical Aspects of Human Sexuality* 11.

Bonaparte, Marie. 1952. "Some Biophysical Aspects of Sadomasochism." *International Journal of Psychoanalysis* 33: 373–84.

Bondurant, Sidney, W., and Stephen C. Cappannari. "Penis Captivity: Fact or Fancy?" *Medical Aspects of Human Sexuality* 5: 224–33.

Braun, Saul, ed. 1975. "S/M." *Catalog of Sexual Consciousness*, pp. 104–9. New York: Grove.

Brown, J. R. W. 1983. "Paraphilias: Sadomasochism, Fetishism, Transvestism, and Transsexuality." *British Journal of Psychiatry* 143: 227–31.

Buhrich, N. 1983. "The Association of Erotic Piercing with Homosexuality, Sadomasochism, Bondage, Fetishism, and Tattoos." *Archives of Sexual Behavior* 12: 167–71.

Califia, Pat. 1979. "Unraveling the Sexual Fringe: A Secret Side of Lesbian Sexuality." *The Advocate* 283: 19–23.

Coburn, Judith. 1977. "S&M." *New Times* 8: 43, 45–50.

Comfort, Alexander. 1974. "Pain/Pleasure." *Forum* 3: 46–49.

———. 1976. "Le Ligotage." *Union* 48: 14–32.

Cordova, Jeanne. 1976. "Towards a Feminist Expression of Sadomasochism." *Lesbian Tide* 6: 14–17.

Davidson, Ralph. 1976. "S/M Comes Out of the Closet." *Forum* 5: 15–17, 20–21.

Demay, Christian. 1975. "Tortures et sexualité." *Union* 37: 12–21.

Denko, Joanne D. 1976. "Klismaphilia—Amplification of the Erotica Enema Device." *American Journal of Psychotherapy* 30: 236–55.

Dietz, Manuel. 1974. "Cruelty in Sex." *Human Response* 1: 7–10.

Droit, Roger-Pol, and Antoine Gallien. 1974. "Un Couple témoigné." *Union* 26: 6–17.

Eulenberg, Albert. 1934. *Algolagnia: The Psychology, Neurology, and Physiology of Sadistic Love and Masochism.* New York: New Era.

Fenichel, Otto. 1925. "The Clinical Aspects of the Need for Punishment." *International Journal of Psychoanalysis* 9: 47–70.

Ferber, Leon. 1975. "Beating Fantasies." *Masturbation from Infancy to Senescence,* ed. I. Marcus and J. Frances, pp. 205–22. New York: International Universities.

G., H. 1968. "The Sadomasochists' Bizarre World of Sexual Pleasure." *Sexology* 40: 54–58.

Geraghty, Tony. 1974. "It Takes All Kinds." *Forum* 3: 55–58.

Gibson, Ian. 1978. *The English Vice: Beating, Sex, and Shame in Victorian England and After.* London: Duckworth.

Haft, Jay Stuart, and H. B. Benjamin. 1973. "Foreign Bodies in the Rectum: Some Psychosocial Aspects." *Medical Aspects of Human Sexuality* 7: 74–95.

Holbrook, M. B. 1986. "A Note on Sadomasochism in the Review Process: I Hate When That Happens." *Journal of Marketing* 50: 104–8.

Horney, Karen. 1946. "Sadistic Love." *Auxiliary Council to the Association for the Advancement of Psychoanalysis.* New York.

"J'aime me faire fouetter." 1976. *Union* 51: 50–58.

Jones, A. 1983. "Coming to Power: Writings and Graphics on Lesbian S/M." *Nation* 236: 667.

Joseph, Edward D., ed. 1965. *Beating Fantasies: Regressive Ego Phenomena in Psychoanalysis.* New York: International Universities.

Josephson, J. 1983. "S/M and Feminism." *Nation* 237: 98.

Karpman, Benjamin. 1946. "Felonious Assault Revealed as a Symptom of Abnormal Sexuality: A Contribution to the Psychogenesis of Psychopathic Behavior." *Journal of Criminal Law and Criminology* 37: 193–215.

Kaunitz, Paul E. 1977. "Sadomasochistic Marriages." *Medical Aspects of Human Sexuality* 11: 66, 68–69, 74, 79–80.

Kaye, B. C. 1975. "Unusual Sex Games for Daring Partners." *Sexology* 41: 48–51.

Keiser, Sylvan. 1949. "The Fear of Sexual Passivity in the Maso-chist." *International Journal of Psychoanalysis* 30: 162–71.

Klein, Henriette. 1972. "Masochism." *Medical Aspects of Human Sexuality* 6: 33–53.

Klimmer, Rudolf. 1972. "Bericht uber einen Masochisten mit homo-sexuellem Einschlag." *Zeitschrift fur arztliche Fortbildung* 66: 782–85.

Kurth, Wolfram. 1976. "Lustgewinn aus Grausamkeit." *Sexual-medizin* 5: 513–16.

Leigh, L. H. 1976. "Sado-masochism, Consent, and the Reform of the Criminal Law." *Modern Law Review* 39: 130–46.

Leppo, Luciano. 1965. "Omosessualita e Masochismo Psichio." *Ses-suologia* 6: 184–86.

Leroy, Bernard. 1908. "Un Singulier cas de perversion sexuelle: La passion des chaines." *Journal de Psychologie Normale et Pathologique* 5: 1–16.

Levitt, Eugene E. 1971. "Sadomasochism." *Sexual Behavior* 1: 68–80.

Levy, Howard S. 1975. "What's Turning Them on in Japan." *Sex-ology* 42: 26–28.

Liaboe, G. P., and J. D. Guy. 1985. "Masochism and the Distortion of Servanthood." *Journal of Psychology and Theology* 13: 255–62.

Lihn, Henry. 1971. "Sexual Masochism: A Case Report." *International Journal of Psychoanalysis* 52: 469–78.

Lister, Milton. 1957. "The Analysis of an Unconscious Beating Fantasy in a Woman." *International Journal of Psychoanalysis* 38: 22–31.

Litman, Robert E., and Charles Swearingen. 1973. " 'Bondage' and Suicide." *Medical Aspects of Human Sexuality* 7: 164–95.

Lowery, Shearon A., and Charles V. Wetl. 1982. "Sexual Asphyxia: A Neglected Area of Study." *Deviant Behavior* 4: 19–39.

Ludovici, Anthony M. 1948. "Untapped Reserves of Sadism in Modern Men and Women." *Journal of Sex Education* 1: 95–100.

Mann, Geoffrey T. 1978. "My Most Unusual Sexual Case—Accidental Strangulation during Sexual Activity." *Medical Aspects of Human Sexuality* 12: 47.

McLeish, John. 1960. "Sadism and Masochism." *Medical World* 93: 363–67.

McNeill, Elizabeth. 1978. *Nine and a Half Weeks: A Memoir of a Love Affair.* New York: Dutton.

Milner, Richard B. 1981. "Orgasm of Death." *Hustler* 8: 33–34.

Mollinger, R. N. 1982. "Sadomasochism and Developmental Stages." *Psychoanalytic Review* 69: 379–89.

Moser, C. 1984. "Against Sadomasochism: A Radical Feminist Analysis." *Journal of Sex Research* 20: 417–19.

Moser, Charles Allen. 1979. "An Exploratory-Descriptive Study of a Self-defined S/M Sample." Ph.D. dissertation, Institute for the Advanced Study of Human Sexuality.

Nichols, Jack. 1979. "Butcher than Thou: Beyond Machismo." *Gay Men: The Sociology of Male Homosexuality*, ed. P. Levine, pp. 328–42. New York: Harper and Row.

"One Couple's S/M Follies." 1977. *Sexology* 43: 44–49, 61, 81.

Park, R. L. 1976. "Irving Klaw: The Godfather of Bondage." *Fetish Times Gazette* 1: 18–21.

Parkin, Alan. 1964. "On Sexual Enthrallment." *Journal of the Psychoanalytic Association* 12: 336–56.

Randell, John B. 1973. "Sadism and Masochism." *Sexual Variations*, pp. 95–102. London: Priory.

Reich, Wilhelm. 1944. "The Masochistic Character." *International Journal of Sex-Economy and Orgone-Research* 3: 38–61.

Revitch, Eugene. 1965. "Extreme Manifestations of Sexual Aggression." *Welfare Reporter* 16: 10–16.

Riccetelli, Anne Marie. 1974. "Sadomasochism—American Style." *Forum* 3: 43–47.

Rich, B. R. 1986. "Against Sadomasochism: A Radical Feminist Analysis." *Feminist Studies* 12: 525–61.

Robertiello, Richard C. 1970. "Masochism and the Female Sexual Role." *Journal of Sex Research* 6: 56–58.

Rothman, G. 1971. *The Riddle of Cruelty*. New York: Philosophical Library.

Rund, Jeffrey Bruce. 1977. "Bizarre: What's in a Word?" *Club* 3: 55–57.

Samois, ed. 1979. *What Color Is Your Handkerchief?* N.p.

Sass, Frank. 1975. "Sexual Asphyxia in the Female." *Journal of Forensic Sciences* 20: 181–85.

Schindler, Walter. 1949. "The Problem of Masochism in Individuals and Nations." *International Journal of Sexology* 2: 167–73.

Socarides, Charles W. 1974. "The Demonified Mother: A Study of Voyeurism and Sexual Sadism." *International Review of Psycho-Analysis* 1: 187–95.

Sonderbo, K., and A. Nyfors. 1986. "Skin-lesions in Sadomasochism." *Dermatologica* 172: 196–200.

Soral, Rene. 1975. "Le Marquis de Sade, precurseur de la libération homosexuelle." *Arcadie* 22: 599–606.

Spengler, Andreas. 1977. "Manifest Sadomasochism of Males: Results of an Empirical Study." *Archives of Sexual Behavior* 6: 441–56.

————. 1979. *Sadomasochisten und ihre Subkulturen*. Frankfurt: Campus Verlag.

Stoller, Robert. 1976. "Sexual Excitement." *Archives of General Psychiatry* 33: 899–909.

Usher, A. 1963. "Accidental Hanging in Relation to Abnormal Sexual Practices." *Newcastle Medical Journal* 27: 234.

Usher, Alan. 1975. "Sexual Violence." *Forensic Science* 5: 243–55.

Van Ophuijsen, J. H. W. 1921. "The Sexual Aim of Sadism as Manifested in Acts of Violence." *International Journal of Psychoanalysis* 10: 139–44.

Verus. 1904. *Kinderprugeln und Sexualtrieb*. Leipzig: Walther Rohmann.

Weinberg, M. S., C. J. Williams, and C. Moser. 1984. "The Social Constituents of Sadomasochism." *Social Problems* 31: 379–89.

Weisman, Avery D. 1967. "Self-Destruction and Sexual Perversion." *Essays in Self-Destruction*, ed. E. S. Shneidman, pp. 265–99. New York: Science House.

Wendt, Herbert. 1965. "The Pleasure of Pain." *The Sex Life of the Animals*, pp. 101–6. New York: Simon and Schuster.

White, Edmund. 1979. "Sado Machismo." *New Times* 13: 54, 57, 58, 60.

"Ein Widerschein von Liebeswirklichkeit: Sadomasochistische Annoncen in Zeitschriften fur Homosexuelle." 1974. *Sexualmedizin* 3: 585–88.

Wiest, J. 1983. "Sadomasochism: Etiology and Treatment." *Clinical Social Work Journal* 11: 292–94.

Young, Ian. 1979. "Sado-masochism." *The New Gay Liberation*, ed. L. Richmond and G. Noguera, pp. 45–53. Palo Alto, Calif.: Ramparts.

S AND M SERIALS

Aching Asses. Published by Fantasy House, P.O. Box 8350, Van Nuys, CA 91409.

Advanced Bondage. Distributed at P.O. Box AE, Dept. 58, Westminster, CA 92683.

Aggressive Women. Published by H.O.M., Inc., P.O. Box 7302, Van Nuys, CA 91409. Contains advertising, personal ads, stories, and feature articles.

Aphrodisia. Published by Esoteric Press, P.O. Box 162, Great Neck, NY 11022.

Ballet Shoes and Boots. Published by Delta Enterprises, P.O. Box 237, Bronx, NY 10462.

B & D Digest. Published quarterly by B & D Publishing Co., P.O. Box 2146, Philadelphia, PA 19103. Contains advertising, personal ads, stories, and feature articles.

B & D Pleasures. Published by B & D Pleasures, P.O. Box 92889, Long Beach, CA 90809–2889. Contains advertising, personal ads, stories, and feature articles.

B & D Quarterly. Distributed by Star Distributors, Ltd., P.O. Box 362, Canal St. Station, New York, NY 10013.

B & D Review. Published by Guide Publications. Distributed by Magazine Service Co., 2424 Newport Boulevard, Suite 113, Costa Mesa, CA 96267. Contains advertising and personal ads.

The Best of Ouch! Published by Matriarch Productions, Box 4295, New York, NY 10017.

Betty Page. Distributed by Star Distributors, Ltd., Box 362, Canal Street Station, New York, NY 10013.

The Big "E." Published by Superlive Productions, Inc., P.O. Box 1260, Ronkonkoma, NY 11779.

Bizarre. Published by Valerie Publications, 204 W. 20th, New York, NY 10011. Contains advertising, personal ads, stories, and feature articles.

Bizarre Fantasies. Distributed by Star Distributors, Ltd., P.O. Box 362, Canal Street Station, New York, NY 10013.

Bizarre Fotos. Distributed by Star Distributors, Ltd., P. O. Box 362, Canal Street Station, New York, NY 10013.

Bizarre Library. Published monthly by CDL, P.O. Box 101, Murray Hill Station, New York, NY 10016. Contains advertising, personal ads, stories, and feature articles.

Bizarre Lifestyles. Published quarterly by Executive Imports, 210 Fifth Avenue, New York, NY 10010. Contains advertising, personal ads, stories, and feature articles.

Black Amazon Digest. Distributed by B & D Digest Club, P.O. Box 2146, Philadelphia, PA 19103.

Black Bondage. Published by Fantasy House, P.O. Box 8350, Van Nuys, CA 91409.

Black Patent. Distributed at P.O. Box AE, Dept. 58, Westminster, CA 92683.

Bondage: An In-Depth Study. Published annually by Eros Publishing Co., Inc., Wilmington, DE. Distributed by Parliament News, Inc., 12011 Sherman Road, North Hollywood, CA 91605. Contains pseudo-scholarly articles.

Bondage Annual. Published by Esoteric Press, P.O. Box 162, Great Neck, NY 11022, and/or by Matriarch Productions, Box 4295, New York, NY 10017.

Bondage Cinema. Published by H.O.M., Inc., P.O. Box 7302, Van Nuys, CA 91409.

Bondage Classics. Published quarterly by H.O.M., Inc., P.O. Box 7302, Van Nuys, CA 91409. Contains advertising and feature articles.

Bondage Folio. Published by H.O.M., Inc., P.O. Box 7302, Van Nuys, CA 91409.

Bondage from Europe. Distributed by Star Distributors, Ltd., P.O. Box 362, Canal Street Station, New York, NY 10013.

Bondage Journal. Published by H.O.M., Inc., P.O. Box 7302, Van Nuys, CA 91409.

Bondage Parade. Published quarterly by London Enterprises, Ltd. Distributed by Lyndon Distributors, Ltd., 15756 Arminta Street, Van Nuys, CA 91406. Contains advertising and stories.

Bondage Revue. Published by H.O.M., Inc., P.O. Box 7302, Van Nuys, CA 91409, and/or distributed by Star Distributors, Ltd., P.O. Box 362, Canal Street Station, New York, NY 10013.

Bondage Times. Published by Superlive Publications, Inc., P.O. Box 362, Canal Street Station, New York, NY 10013.

Bondage World. Distributed by Star Distributors, Ltd., P.O. Box 362, Canal Street Station, New York, NY 10013.

Bottoms Up. Published by Esoteric Press, P.O. Box 162, Great Neck, NY 11022, and/or by Superlive Publications, Inc., P.O. Box 1260, Ronkonkoma, NY 11779.

Bound & Spread. Distributed by Star Distributors, Ltd., P.O. Box 362, Canal Street Station, New York, NY 10013.

Bound to Please. Published by H.O.M. Publications, P.O. Box 7302, Van Nuys, CA 91409. Contains advertisements and stories.

Bound to Serve. Published by London Enterprises, Ltd., 15756 Arminta Street, Van Nuys, CA 91406.

Breast Bondage. Published by H.O.M., Inc., P.O. Box 7302, Van Nuys, CA 91409. Contains advertising and stories.

Burnt Ass. Published by H.O.M., Inc., P.O. Box 7302, Van Nuys, CA 91409.

Captured! Published by H.O.M., Inc., P.O. Box 7302, Van Nuys, CA 91409.

Catalogue of Sensual and Exotic Sexual Devices and Appliances. Published by Esoteric Press, P.O. Box 162, Great Neck, NY 11022.

Catspats. Distributed by Janus, Box 125, 6752 Fourth Avenue, Brooklyn, NY 11220. Contains advertising and photos.

Centurians. Published by Matriarch Productions, Box 4295, New York, NY 10017, and/or distributed at P.O. Box AE, Dept. 58, Westminster, CA 92683. Contains advertising, stories, and feature articles.

Classic Bondage. Distributed by Star Distributors, Ltd., P.O. Box 362, Canal Street Station, New York, NY 10013.

Club. Published monthly by Fiona Press, Inc., P.O. Box 6100, Newtown, CT 0647. Contains advertising, personal ads, stories, and feature articles.

The Collection of Wet. Published by Superlive Productions, Inc., P.O. Box 1260, Ronkonkoma, NY 11779.

The Collective Works of Kane Photos. Distributed by Star Distributors, Ltd., P.O. Box 362, Canal Street Station, New York, NY 10013.

The Complete House of Leather Restraints Catalog. Published by House of Milan Corp., P.O. Box 25304, Chicago, IL 60625.

Corporal. Published by Esoteric Press, Inc., P.O. Box 30482, JFK Station, Jamaica, NY 11430. Contains advertising, personal ads, stories, and feature articles. Newspaper stock, but advertised in *Lisa's World* (see below) as "now in magazine form" with the following address: Esoteric Press, P.O. Box 162, Great Neck, NY 11022.

Countess Anne: Mistress of Pain. Published by Fantasy House, P.O. Box 8350, Van Nuys, CA 91409.

Custom Shoe Catalog. Published by Delta Enterprises, P.O. Box 237, Bronx, NY 10462.

Deviations. Published by Matriarch Productions, Box 4295, New York, NY 10017.

Dial Your Mistress. Published by Superlive Productions, Inc., P.O. Box 1260, Ronkonkoma, NY 11779.

Disclipine Classes for Unruly Slaves. Published by Matriarch Productions, Box 4295, New York, NY 10017.

Discipline Helmets. Published by Matriarch Productions, Box 4295, New York, NY 10017.

Do-It-Yourself Tit & Body Torture. Distributed by Star Distributors, Ltd., P.O. Box 362, Canal Street Station, New York, NY 10013.

Dominated and Diapered. Distributed by Star Distributors, Ltd., P.O. Box 362, Canal Street Station, New York, NY 10013.

Dominatrix Domain. Published by Matriarch Productions, Box 4295, New York, NY 10017, and by Superlive Productions, Inc., P.O. Box 1260, Ronkonkoma, NY 11779.

Enema Erotica. Published by Superlive Productions, Inc., P.O. Box 1260, Ronkonkoma, NY 11779.

Enema Games. Published by Superlive Productions, Inc., P.O. Box 1260, Ronkonkoma, NY 11779.

Enema Resort. Published by Superlive Productions, Inc., P.O. Box 1260, Ronkonkoma, NY 11779.

Enema Thrills. Published by Superlive Productions, Inc., P.O. Box 1260, Ronkonkoma, NY 11779.

Enslave. Published by Esoteric Press, P.O. Box 162, Great Neck, NY 11022.

Erotic Bondage. Distributed at P.O. Box AE, Dept. 58, Westminster, CA 92683.

Executive Imports Catalogs. Published by Executive Imports, 210 Fifth Avenue, New York, NY 10010. Contains advertising and personal ads.

Exotic High Heels. Published by Delta Enterprises, P.O. Box 237, Bronx, NY 10462.

Exotic Platform Shoes and Boots. Published by Delta Enterprises, P.O. Box 237, Bronx, NY 10462.

Exotique. Published by Fantasy House, P.O. Box 8350, Van Nuys, CA 91409.

The Faithful Servant. Published by Fantasy House, P.O. Box 8350, Van Nuys, CA 91409.

Fantasia. Distributed at P.O. Box AE, Dept. 58, Westminster, CA 92683.

Fantasy Fulfillment Newsletter. Published by Arcadia Enterprises, 200 Park Avenue, Suite 303E, New York, NY 10017.

Fantasy Register. Distributed by Star Distributors, Ltd., P.O. Box 362, Canal Street Station, New York, NY 10013.

Female Supremacy. Published by Superlive Productions, Inc., P.O. Box 1260, Ronkonkoma, NY 11779.

Femme Fatale. Published quarterly by Arcadia Enterprises, 200 Park Avenue, Suite 303E, New York, NY 10017. Contains advertising, personal ads, stories, and feature articles.

Fetish Fantasies. Contains advertising, stories, and feature articles.

Fetish Films Quarterly. Distributed by Star Distributors, Ltd., P.O. Box 362, Canal Street Station, New York, NY 10013.

Flaming Bottoms. Published by Superlive Productions, Inc., P.O. Box 1260, Ronkonkoma, NY 11779.

For Unruly Slaves. Published by Superlive Productions, Inc., P.O. Box 1260, Ronkonkoma, NY 11779.

Get Kinky. Published by Modern Publications, P.O. Box 3636, Fort Pierce, FL 33448.

Glamour in Bondage. Distributed by Star Distributors, Ltd., P.O. Box 362, Canal Street Station, New York, NY 10013.

High Heeled Boots. Published by Delta Enterprises, P.O. Box 237, Bronx, NY 10462.

High Heels. Published by Fantasy House, P.O. Box 8350, Van Nuys, CA 91409.

Hogtie. Published by H.O.M., Inc., P.O. Box 7302, Van Nuys, CA 91409.

Hospital Restraints. Published by Matriarch Productions, Box 4295, New York, NY 10017.

Hot Cheeks. Published by Superlive Productions, Inc., P.O. Box 1260, Ronkonkoma, NY 11779.

Humbly Yours. Published by Superlive Productions, Inc., P.O. Box 1260, Ronkonkoma, NY 11779.

Kane Photo Bondage. Distributed by Star Distributors, Ltd., P.O. Box 362, Canal Street Station, New York, NY 10013.

Kidnaped! Published by H.O.M., Inc., P.O. Box 7302, Van Nuys, CA 91409. Contains advertising and stories.

Kinky Kontacts: For Fetish Lovers Only. Superlative Publications, Inc., P.O. Box 1260, Ronkonkoma, NY 11779. Contains advertising, personal ads, stories, and feature articles.

Knotty. Published by H.O.M., Inc., P.O. Box 7302, Van Nuys, CA 91409.

K.P. Exchange. Distributed by Star Distributors, Ltd., P.O. Box 362, Canal Street Station, New York, NY 10013.

Latent Image. Published by H.O.M., Inc., P.O. Box 7302, Van Nuys, CA 91409.

Leather Bondage. Distributed at P.O. Box AE, Dept. 58, Westminster, CA 92683.

Leather Restraint. Published by H.O.M., Inc., P.O. Box 7302, Van Nuys, CA 91409.

Lesbian Enema Lovers. Published by Superlive Productions, Inc., P.O. Box 1260, Ronkonkoma, NY 11779.

Letters. Published ten times per year by Letters Magazine, Inc., P.O. Box 1314, Teaneck, NJ 07666. Contains advertising and letters from readers.

Lisa's World. Published by Esoteric Press, Inc., P.O. Box 162, Great Neck, NY 11022. Contains advertising, personal ads, stories, and feature articles.

Love Bound. Published by Superlive Productions, Inc., P.O. Box 1260, Ronkonkoma, NY 11779.

Love Unlimited. P.O. Box 15203, Columbus, OH 43215. Contains advertising, personal ads, and feature articles.

Maids and Mistresses. Published by Fantasy House, P.O. Box 8350, Van Nuys, CA 91409.

Maitresse. Published by Matriarch Productions, Box 4295, New York, NY 10017.

Male Bondage. Published by London Enterprises, Ltd., 15756 Arminta Street, Van Nuys, CA 91406. Contains advertising and stories.

Master's Digest. Published by H.O.M., Inc., P.O. Box 7302, Van Nuys, CA 91409.

Mediaeval. Distributed at P.O. Box AE, Dept. 58, Westminster, CA 92683.

Mistress of Pain. Contains stories and photos.

Movie Photo Packs. Distributed by Star Distributors, Ltd., P.O. Box 362, Canal Street Station, New York, NY 10013.

Naked Bondage. Published by H.O.M., Inc., P.O. Box 7302, Van Nuys, CA 91409.

Nostalgia. Distributed at P.O. Box AE, Dept. 58, Westminster, CA 92683.

Obeah: Society of Black Masters & Mistresses. Distributed by Star Distributors, Ltd., P.O. Box 362, Canal Street Station, New York, NY 10013.

Obedience! Published by H.O.M., Inc., P.O. Box 7302, Van Nuys, CA 91409.

Obeisance. Distributed by Star Distributors, Ltd., P.O. Box 362, Canal Street Station, New York, NY 10013.

Painful Pleasures. Published by Esoteric Press, P.O. Box 162, Great Neck, NY 11022.

Patent Clothing Catalog. Published by Esoteric Press, P.O. Box 162, Great Neck, NY 11022.

Penthouse Variations. Published monthly by Viva International, Ltd., 21st Floor, 909 Third Avenue, New York, NY 10022. Contains advertising, stories, and feature articles.

Petticoat Power. Published by Matriarch Productions, Box 4295, New York, NY 10017.

Pleasure Parade. Published by Eric Stanton, P.O. Box 163, Gracie Station, New York, NY 10028. Contains cartoons.

Punished! Published by H.O.M., Inc., P.O. Box 7302, Van Nuys, CA 91409. Contains advertising and stories.

Red Patent: Leather Bondage. Distributed at P.O. Box AE, Dept. 58, Westminster, CA 92683.

Restrained. Published by Superlive Productions, Inc., P.O. Box 1260, Ronkonkoma, NY 11779.

Rubber Bondage. Distributed at P.O. Box AE, Dept. 58, Westminster, CA 92683.

The Satin Factory. Published by Esoteric Press, P.O. Box 162, Great Neck, NY 11022.

Serana. Published by H.O.M., Inc., P.O. Box 7302, Van Nuys, CA 91409.

7" Shoes and Boots. Published by Delta Enterpises, P.O. Box 237, Bronx, NY 10462.

Shaved Bondage. Published by Fantasy House, P.O. Box 8350, Van Nuys, CA 91409.

She-Fights! Distributed by Star Distributors, Ltd., P.O. Box 362, Canal Street Station, New York, NY 10013.

She . . . Who Must Be Obeyed. Distributed by Star Distributors, Ltd., P.O. Box 362, Canal Street Station, New York, NY 10013.

Slap Shots. Published by Superlive Productions, Inc., P.O. Box 1260, Ronkonkoma, NY 11779.

Slave Exchange. Published by Esoteric Press, Inc., P.O. Box 162, Great Neck, NY 11022. Contains advertising, personal ads, stories, and feature articles.

Slave of Lust. Contains stories and photos.

SM Express. Mole Publishing, 1282 N. Lake Street, #104, Aurora, IL 60507. Contains advertising, personal ads, stories, and feature articles.

Spank Hard. Published by Superlive Productions, Inc., P.O. Box 1260, Ronkonkoma, NY 11779.

Spanking Times. Published by Superlive Productions, Inc., P.O. Box 1260, Ronkonkoma, NY 11779.

Stalked! Published by H.O.M., Inc., P.O. Box 7302, Van Nuys, CA 91409.

Stays & Gloves. Published by Esoteric Press, P.O. Box 162, Great Neck, NY 11022.

Strict! Distributed by Star Distributors, Ltd., P.O. Box 362, Canal Street Station, New York, NY 10013.

Submit. Published by Esoteric Press, P.O. Box 162, Great Neck, NY 11022.

Suspended! Published by H.O.M., Inc., P.O. Box 7302, Van Nuys, CA 91409. Contains advertising and stories.

Sweet Submission. Published by Carter Stevens/Matriarch Publications, 153 W. 24th Street, New York, NY 10011. Contains advertising, stories, and feature articles.

Taskmaster. Published quarterly by BB Publications, 5464 Santa Monica Boulevard, Los Angeles, CA 90028. Contains advertising and feature articles.

3 Dominatrixes. Distributed by Star Distributors, Ltd., P.O. Box 362, Canal Street Station, New York, NY 10013.

Tied & Tickled. Distributed by Star Distributors, Ltd., P.O. Box 362, Canal Street Station, New York, NY 10013.

Tight Ropes. Published by H.O.M., Inc., P.O. Box 7302, Van Nuys, CA 91409.

Trainers & Gags. Published by Matriarch Productions, Box 4295, New York, NY 10017.

TV Times. Published by Superlive Productions, Inc., P.O. Box 1260, Ronkonkoma, NY 11779.

29 Photo Packs. Published by H.O.M., Inc., P.O. Box 7302, Van Nuys, CA 91409.

269 Wet Photos. Published by Superlive Productions, Inc., P.O. Box 1260, Ronkonkoma, NY 11779.

235 Bondage Photos. Published by Superlive Productions, Inc., P.O. Box 1260, Ronkonkoma, NY 11779.

Vampirella. Contains cartoons.

Vibrations. Published monthly by David Zentner/Vanity Publishing Co., 60 East 42nd Street, New York, NY 10165. Contains advertising, stories, feature articles, and letters from readers.

Water & Power. Published by Superlive Productions, Inc., P.O. Box 1260, Ronkonkoma, NY 11779.

Waterpower. Published by Superlive Productions, Inc., P.O. Box 1260, Ronkonkoma, NY 11779.

Waterworks. Published by Superlive Productions, Inc., P.O. Box 1260, Ronkonkoma, NY 11779.

Wet Fantasies. Published by Superlive Productions, Inc., P.O. Box 1260, Ronkonkoma, NY 11779.

Wet Films. Published by Superlive Productions, Inc., P.O. Box 1260, Ronkonkoma, NY 11779.

Wet Letters. Published by Superlive Productions, Inc., P.O. Box 1260, Ronkonkoma, NY 11779.

Whip Maid. Distributed at P.O. Box AE, Dept. 58, Westminster, CA 92683.

Whipmaster. Published by H.O.M., Inc., P.O. Box 7302, Van Nuys, CA 91409. Contains advertising, stories, and feature articles.

White Patent. Distributed at P.O. Box AE, Dept. 58, Westminster, CA 92683.

Women in Command. Published by Star Maker Publications, P.O. Box 289, Canal Street Station, New York, NY 10013. Contains advertising, personal ads, stories, and feature articles.

Women in Tit Torture. Published by Superlive Productions, Inc., P.O. Box 1260, Ronkonkoma, NY 11779.

Index to Synonyms

Although all synonymic relationships are cross-referenced in the glossary, here we present a concise index to all synonyms in the language of sadomasochism.

A: amazon

amazon: A

amazon (2): bitch goddess, discipliness, dominant bitch, dominatrix, dominatrix bitch, female dominant, femdom, goddess, headmistress, mastix, mistress, queen

animal sex: bestiality

arts: love arts

ass plug: butt plug

backgammon: G, Gr, GR, Greek, Greek arts, Greek culture

back parlor: back yard

back yard: back parlor

bad boy: naughty boy

b & d: B & D, b and d, B and D, bd, BD, b/d, B/D, B.D., bondage and discipline, Burgers and Dogs

B & D: b & d, b and d, B and D, bd, BD, b/d, B/D, B.D., bondage and discipline, Burgers and Dogs

b and d: b & d, B & D, B and D, bd, BD, b/d, B/D, B.D., bondage and discipline, Burgers and Dogs

B and D: b & d, B & D,

b and d, bd, BD, b/d, B/D, B.D., bondage and discipline, Burgers and Dogs

bd: b & d, B & D, b and d, B and D, BD, b/d, B/D, B.D., bondage and discipline, Burgers and Dogs

BD: b & d, B & D, b and d, B and D, b/d, B/D, B.D., bondage and discipline, Burgers and Dogs

b/d: b & d, B & D, b and d, B and D, bd, BD, B.D., bondage and discipline, Burgers and Dogs

B/D: b & d, B & D, b and d, B and D, bd, BD, b/d, B.D., bondage and discipline, Burgers and Dogs

B.D.: b & d, B & D, b and d, B and D, bd, BD, b/d, B/D, bondage and discipline, Burgers and Dogs

bestiality: animal sex

bi: bisexual

bitch goddess: amazon (2), discipliness, dominant bitch, dominatrix, dominatrix bitch, female dominant, femdom, goddess, headmistress, mastix, mistress, queen

bondage: burgundy handkerchief

bondage and discipline: b & d, B & D, b and d, B and D, bd, BD, b/d, B/D, B.D., Burgers and Dogs

Boston tea party: brown shower, BS, B/S, hot turds, scat

bottom: M (2), masochist, passive, right hip pocket, S (3), slave (n), sub, submissive

breast torture: nipple bon-

dage, nipple breast bondage, nipple discipline, nipple restraint, nipple torture, nt, tit bondage, tit discipline, tit torture, titty bondage, titty discipline, titty torture, tt

brown shower: Boston tea party, BS, B/S, hot turds, scat

BS: Boston tea party, brown shower, B/S, hot turds, scat

B/S: Boston tea party, brown shower, BS, hot turds, scat

bull bitch: she-male (2)

Burgers and Dogs: b & d, B & D, b and d, B and D, bd, BD, b/d, B/D, B.D., bondage and discipline

burgundy handkerchief: bondage

butt plug: ass plug

CA: C/A, C.A., CD, C/D, C.D., corporal arts, corporal discipline, corporal punishment, CP, C/P, C.P.

C/A: CA, C.A., CD, C/D, C.D., corporal arts, corporal discipline, corporal punishment, CP, C/P, C.P.

C.A.: CA, C/A, CD, C/D, C.D., corporal arts, corporal discipline, corporal punishment, CP, C/P, C.P.

C & B torture: cock and ball torture

candle wax torture: hot wax, wax, wax torture

cat (n): cat-o-nine-tails

cat (v): cat-fighting

cat-fighting: cat (v)

cat-o-nine-tails: cat (n)

CD: CA, C/A, C.A., C/D, C.D., corporal arts, corporal dis-

femdom, goddess, head-
mistress, mastix, mistress,
queen

dominatrix bitch: amazon (2),
bitch goddess, discipliness,
dominant bitch, domina-
trix, female dominant,
femdom, goddess, head-
mistress, mastix, mistress,
queen

dual: middle, switchable

dungeon: mardi gras room,
playroom, training room

E: enema

enema: E

enema discipline: forced circulation, forced enema,
forced fluid injection, forced
lavage, liquid punishment,
liquid torture

English: English arts, English culture, English vice

English arts: English, English culture, English vice

English bracelet: English harness C/R, pin prick C/R,
spike bracelet, studded
bracelet, studded cockring

English cock harness: cock
harness

English culture: English,
English arts, English vice

English harness C/R: English
bracelet, pin prick C/R,
spike bracelet, studded
bracelet, studded cockring

English vice: English, English
arts, English culture

entertain: host

equestrian: equestrian
training

equestrian training: equestrian

equipment: toys

extended ritual: prolonged ritual, prolonged scene, protracted ritual

F: fr, FR, French, French
art(s), French culture(s)

face-sitting: heavy squatting,
queening

FD: female dominance

female dominance: FD

female dominant: amazon (2),
bitch goddess, discipliness,
dominant bitch, domina-
trix, dominatrix bitch,
femdom, goddess, head-
mistress, mastix, mistress,
queen

femdom: amazon (2), bitch
goddess, discipliness, dominant bitch, dominatrix,
dominatrix bitch, female
dominant, goddess, head-
mistress, mastix, mistress,
queen

ff: fistfuck (ing), fist (ing),
handball (ing), handfuck
(ing)

finger dose: finger wave

finger wave: finger dose

fist (ing):   ff, fistfuck (ing),
handball (ing), handfuck
(ing)

fistfuck (ing):   ff, fist (ing),
handball (ing), handfuck
(ing)

forced circulation: enema discipline, forced enema,
forced fluid injection, forced
lavage, liquid punishment,
liquid torture

forced enema: enema discipline, forced circulation,
forced fluid injection, forced
lavage, liquid punishment,
liquid torture

forced fluid injection: enema
discipline, forced circulation, forced enema, forced
lavage, liquid punishment,
liquid torture

forced French: forced oral, oral servitude, oral worship

forced Greek: ramming

forced lavage: enema discipline, forced circulation, forced enema, forced fluid injection, liquid punishment, liquid torture

forced oral: forced French, oral servitude, oral worship

fr: F, FR, French, French art(s), French culture(s)

FR: F, fr, French, French art(s), French culture(s)

French: F, fr, FR, French art(s), French culture(s)

French art(s): F, fr, FR, French, French culture(s)

French culture(s): F, fr, FR, French, French art(s)

fuck me shoes: high heels

G: backgammon, Gr, GR, Greek, Greek arts, Greek culture

goddess: amazon (2), bitch goddess, discipliness, dominant bitch, dominatrix, dominatrix bitch, female dominant, femdom, headmistress, mastix, mistress, queen

golden nuggets: gold nuggets

golden shower: GS, G/S, G.S., pee fun, pissing

gold nuggets: golden nuggets

Gr: backgammon, G, GR, Greek, Greek arts, Greek culture

GR: backgammon, G, Gr, Greek, Greek arts, Greek culture

Greek: backgammon, G, Gr, GR, Greek arts, Greek culture

Greek arts: backgammon, G, Gr, GR, Greek, Greek culture

Greek culture: backgammon, G, Gr, GR, Greek, Greek arts

GS: golden shower, G/S, G.S., pee fun, pissing

G/S: golden shower, GS, G.S., pee fun, pissing

G.S.: golden shower, GS, G/S, pee fun, pissing

H: humiliation

handball (ing): ff, fistfuck (ing), fist (ing), handfuck (ing)

handfuck (ing): ff, fistfuck (ing), fist (ing), handball (ing)

headmistress: amazon (2), bitch goddess, discipliness, dominant bitch, dominatrix, dominatrix bitch, female dominant, femdom, goddess, mastix, mistress, queen

heavy squatting: face-sitting, queening

high heel discipline: high heel training, spike action, trampling

high heels: fuck me shoes

high heel training: high heel discipline, spike action, trampling

host: entertain

hot turds: Boston tea party, brown shower, BS, B/S, scat

hot wax: candle wax torture, wax, wax torture

housemaid: maid

humble: humiliate

humiliate: humble

humiliation: H

kennel discipline: doggie, kennel training

kennel training: doggie, kennel discipline

key-word: safe word

kitty: mini cat

leather: leather/rubber, leather scene, leather sex, L/R

leather bath: leather club

leather club: leather bath

leather man (2):   leather queen

leather queen: leather man (2)

leather/rubber: leather, leather scene, leather sex, L/R

leather scene: leather, leather/ rubber, leather sex, L/R

leather sex: leather, leather/ rubber, leather scene, L/R

left hip pocket: corporalist, dom, dominant, M (3), master, S (2), sadist, sender, sir, taskmaster, top

liquid punishment: enema discipline, forced circulation, forced enema, forced fluid injection, forced lavage, liquid torture

liquid torture: enema discipline, forced circulation, forced enema, forced fluid injection, forced lavage, liquid punishment

love arts: arts

L/R: leather, leather/rubber, leather scene, leather sex

M (1):   masochism, pagan worship

M (2):   bottom, masochist, passive, right hip pocket, S (3), slave (n), sub, submissive

M (3):   corporalist, dom, dominant, left hip pocket, master, S (2), sadist, sender, sir, taskmaster, top

maid: housemaid

mardi gras room: dungeon, playroom, training room

masochism: M (1), pagan worship

masochist: bottom, M (2), passive, right hip pocket, S (3), slave (n), sub, submissive

master: corporalist, dom, dominant, left hip pocket, M (3), S (2), sadist, sender, sir, taskmaster, top

mastix: amazon (2), bitch goddess, discipliness, dominant bitch, dominatrix, dominatrix bitch, female dominant, femdom, goddess, headmistress, mistress, queen

middle: dual, switchable

mini cat: kitty

mistress: amazon (2), bitch goddess, discipliness, dominant bitch, dominatrix, dominatrix bitch, female dominant, femdom, goddess, headmistress, mastix, queen

naughty boy: bad boy

nipple bondage: breast torture, nipple breast bondage, nipple discipline, nipple restraint, nipple torture, nt, tit bondage, tit discipline, tit torture, titty bondage, titty discipline, titty torture, tt

nipple breast bondage: breast

torture, nipple bondage, nipple discipline, nipple restraint, nipple torture, nt, tit bondage, tit discipline, tit torture, titty bondage, titty discipline, titty torture, tt

nipple cuff: nipple ring

nipple discipline: breast torture, nipple bondage, nipple breast bondage, nipple restraint, nipple torture, nt, tit bondage, tit discipline, tit torture, titty bondage, titty discipline, titty torture, tt

nipple restraint: breast torture, nipple bondage, nipple breast bondage, nipple discipline, nipple torture, nt, tit bondage, tit discipline, tit torture, titty bondage, titty discipline, titty torture, tt

nipple ring: nipple cuff

nipple torture: breast torture, nipple bondage, nipple breast bondage, nipple discipline, nipple restraint, nt, tit bondage, tit discipline, tit torture, titty bondage, titty discipline, titty torture, tt

nt: breast torture, nipple bondage, nipple breast bondage, nipple discipline, nipple restraint, nipple torture, tit bondage, tit discipline, tit torture, titty bondage, titty discipline, titty torture, tt

obedience training: sex-training, training

oral servitude: forced French, forced oral, oral worship

oral worship: forced French, forced oral, oral servitude

pagan worship: M (1), masochism

party: Roman, Roman arts, Roman culture

passive: bottom, M (2), masochist, right hip pocket, S (3), slave (n), sub, submissive

pb: penis bondage, penis punishment, penis torture, pp, pt

pee fun: golden shower, GS, G/S, G.S., pissing

penis bondage: pb, penis punishment, penis torture, pp, pt

penis punishment: pb, penis bondage, penis torture, pp, pt

penis torture: pb, penis bondage, penis punishment, pp, pt

petticoat discipline: petticoat dressing, petticoat punishment

petticoat dressing: petticoat discipline, petticoat punishment

petticoat punishment: petticoat discipline, petticoat dressing

pickle: red (1)

pin prick C/R: English bracelet, English harness C/R, spike bracelet, studded bracelet, studded cockring

pissing: golden shower, GS, G/S, G.S., pee fun

playroom: dungeon, mardi gras room, training room

pony: pony slave

pony slave: pony

pp: pb, penis bondage, penis

punishment, penis torture, pt

prolonged ritual: extended ritual, prolonged scene, protracted ritual

prolonged scene: extended ritual, prolonged ritual, protracted ritual

protracted ritual: extended ritual, prolonged ritual, prolonged scene

pt: pb, penis bondage, penis punishment, penis torture, pp

punishment helmet: punishment hood

punishment hood: punishment helmet

queen: amazon (2), bitch goddess, discipliness, dominant bitch, dominatrix, dominatrix bitch, female dominant, femdom, goddess, headmistress, mastix, mistress

queening: face-sitting, heavy squatting

ramming: forced Greek

real: true

real masochism: true masochism

real masochist: true masochist

real sadism: true sadism

real sadist: true sadist

red (1):   pickle

reward (1):   rewards of worship

rewards of worship: reward (1)

right hip pocket: bottom, M (2), masochist, passive, S

(3), slave (*n*), sub, submissive

Roman: party, Roman arts, Roman culture

Roman arts: party, Roman, Roman culture

Roman culture: party, Roman, Roman arts

S (1):   sadism

S (2):   corporalist, dom, dominant, left hip pocket, M (3), master, sadist, sender, sir, taskmaster, top

S (3):   bottom, M (2), masochist, passive, right hip pocket, slave (*n*), submissive

sadism: S (1)

sadist: corporalist, dom, dominant, left hip pocket, M (3), master, S (2), sender, sir, taskmaster, top

sadomasochism: S and M, SM, S/M, S-M, S.M., Spaghetti and Macaroni

safe: clean

safe word: key-word

S and M: sadomasochism, SM, S/M, S-M, S.M., Spaghetti and Macaroni

scat: Boston tea party, brown shower, BS, B/S, hot turds

scenario: scene, script

scene: scenario, script

script: scenario, scene

sender: corporalist, dom, dominant, left hip pocket, M (3), master, S (2), sadist, sir, taskmaster, top

sextrain: train

sextraining: obedience training, training

she-male (2):   bull bitch

sir: corporalist, dom, domi-

nipple bondage, nipple breast bondage, nipple discipline, nipple restraint, nipple torture, nt, tit bondage, tit discipline, tit torture, titty discipline, titty torture, tt

titty discipline: breast torture, nipple bondage, nipple breast bondage, nipple discipline, nipple restraint, nipple torture, nt, tit bondage, tit discipline, tit torture, titty bondage, titty torture, tt

titty torture: breast torture, nipple bondage, nipple breast bondage, nipple discipline, nipple restraint, nipple torture, nt, tit bondage, tit discipline, tit torture, titty bondage, titty discipline, tt

toilet: toilet slave

toilet service: toilet servitude, toilet sex, toilet training

toilet servitude: toilet service, toilet sex, toilet training

toilet sex: toilet service, toilet servitude, toilet training

toilet slave: toilet

toilet training: toilet service, toilet servitude, toilet sex

token: token of sincerity

token of sincerety: token

top: corporalist, dom, dominant, left hip pocket, M (3), master, S (2), sadist, sender, sir, taskmaster

toys: equipment

trading: slave exchange, time buying

train: sextrain

training: obedience training, sextraining

training room: dungeon, mardi gras room, playroom

trampling: high heel discipline, high heel training, spike action

transvestite: TV, T.V.

true: real

true masochism: real masochism

true masochist: real masochist

true sadism: real sadism

true sadist: real sadist

tt: breast torture, nipple bondage, nipple breast bondage, nipple discipline, nipple restraint, nipple torture, nt, tit bondage, tit discipline, tit torture, titty bondage, titty discipline, titty torture

tutor: teacher

TV: transvestite, T.V.

TV discipline: TV training

TV training: TV discipline

T.V.:   transvestite, TV

velvet rope: crotch rope

watersports: wet sex, WS, W/ S, W.S.

wax: candle wax torture, hot wax, wax torture

wax torture: candle wax torture, hot wax, wax

wayout: weirdo

weirdo: wayout

wet sex: watersports, WS, W/ S, W.S.

whip (1):   switch (n), whip stick, whipcord

whip (2):   switch (v)

whipcord: switch, whip (1), whip stick

About the Authors

THOMAS E. MURRAY is a professor in the department of English at Kansas State University. Among his publications are *The Language of St. Louis, Missouri*; *Aspects of American English*; *The Language of Handspinning*; *Dialogue Graffiti in American English*; and articles in *American Speech*, *Names*, *SECOL Review*, *Maledicta*, and other journals.

THOMAS R. MURRELL is currently working on a Ph.D. in Twentieth Century American Literature at Ohio State University.